The World Crisis and American Responsibility

Nine Essays
by REINHOLD NIEBUHR

Collected and Edited by
ERNEST W. LEFEVER

GREENWOOD PRESS, PUBLISHERS
WESTPORT, CONNECTICUT

Library of Congress Cataloging in Publication Data

Niebuhr, Reinhold, 1892-1971.
  The world crisis and American responsibility.

  Reprint of the ed. published by Association Press,
New York, in series: A Reflection book.
  1. United States--Relations (general) with foreign
relations--Addresses, essays, lectures. 2. World
politics--1945-   --Addresses, essays, lectures.
I. Title.
[E744.N53 1974]   327.73   74-10643
ISBN 0-8371-7649-2

Originally published in 1958 by the Associaiton Press,
New York

Repirnted with the permission of The National Board of
YMCA's Association Press

Reprinted in 1974 by Greenwood Press, Inc.,
51 Riverside Avenue, Westport, CT 06880

Library of Congress catalog card number 74-10643
ISBN 0-8371-7649-2

Printed in the United States of America

10 9 8 7 6 5 4 3 2

Niebuhr and the World Crisis

by Ernest W. Lefever

Reinhold Niebuhr is widely regarded as America's leading theologian and political philosopher. He is also a preacher and a prophet. Arthur Schlesinger, Jr., has said of him: "No man has had as much influence as a preacher in this generation; no preacher has had as much influence in the secular world."

Perhaps Niebuhr's greatest single contribution to American life and thought has been his interpretation of the crisis that has gripped the world since the beginning of the present century. His understanding of the crisis has taken on added meaning as it became increasingly apparent that history had conferred upon the United States the major responsibility for defending the cherished values of Western civilization.

If it is true that authentic prophets arise when there is a grave political crisis and when there is an assortment of false interpreters of the crisis,

3

the past three decades were made to order for
Reinhold Niebuhr.

The crisis that shook the world when the young
pastor in Detroit first started to preach, and
which still shakes it, is profoundly political and
profoundly religious. The false interpreters of
the crisis who were the targets of Niebuhr's
criticism then and now are religious leaders who
misunderstand the larger meaning of world politics because they misunderstand the larger meaning of the religious tradition from which they
presume to speak.

Niebuhr's restless pen has always pointed in
two directions. It always points straight to the
center of the political issue he is discussing and
it always points to the errors of the "rational-
idealists" or "simple moralists" who compound
the crises with their confusion. In fact, one can
perhaps best gain an understanding of Niebuhr's
views on political morality by studying the criticism he makes of those persons who, in his view,
misunderstand our moral responsibility as citizens and as a nation because they fail to understand the realities of politics.

The wicked prophets, men motivated by evil
designs, are of little interest to Niebuhr. He is
concerned in the main with false prophets. He

directs his frank and powerful polemics against men with noble intentions who, instead of being as wise as serpents, are as harmless as doves and as stupid as chickens. The political irrelevance and moral irresponsibility of the "children of light," he says, is a result of their virtue, their desire to be pure and right. Herein lies its irony. Irony is not an accidental twist of fate that spells catastrophe, but a hidden defect in virtue which promotes the triumph of disaster.

The advice given by American churches and religious leaders on political issues, Niebuhr repeatedly asserts, tends to be "either so irrelevant or so dangerous that a wise statesman will do well to ignore" most of it. Such statesmen can thank God, he adds, that the advice from one source cancels out the advice from another source sufficiently "to make their indifference politically expedient."

In religious circles in the United States and abroad Niebuhr is a controversial figure. He is both praised and criticized, but he is never ignored. In 1953 *The Christian Century*, whose editorial policy Niebuhr has so frequently and sharply attacked over the years, had this to say about him: "For the past 25 years he has alternately assailed many of the most cherished assumptions of American Christianity and instructed it in a better way."

Niebuhr can be called a true prophet because he speaks from a tradition that takes history (and therefore politics) seriously. He always sees the specific event, perhaps tragic in itself, as a part of a larger drama which is neither wholly tragic nor wholly heroic, but which stands under the mercy and judgment of Almighty God. There are elements of hope and tragedy in every human situation. From this perspective he charts a morally sensitive and politically realistic course between the banalities of the utopian moralists and the gloomy dirges of the cynics.

Along with his penetrating critique of the theoretical underpinnings of modern culture and of the emptiness of popular piety, Niebuhr has constructed the most comprehensive and convincing restatement of the Christian interpretation of man and history in our time. One would have to go back to Abraham Lincoln to find the rare combination of political wisdom and moral sensitivity found in this Protestant preacher.

According to Niebuhr's world view, struggle and conflict are permanent features of the international landscape in a world of many nation-states. The incessant struggle of power and purpose is rooted deeply in the selfish drives of men projected from the position of national power. The government of the nation-state is and must be the primary agent of political decision and moral responsibility in world politics. The existence of international instruments like the United Nations, he maintains, does not change the basic realities of international affairs, although such instruments may be used by nation-states to mitigate and redirect conflict.

Niebuhr's political realism is not the sham realism of the cynic who sees only the stupidity and wickedness of man and gives up in despair. His realism is that of a man of humility who sees both the limitations and the possibilities of human nature. In a classic statement Niebuhr once said: "Man's capacity for justice makes democracy possible; but man's inclination to injustice makes democracy necessary." He believes that America has the basic spiritual, cultural, economic and political resources to respond with understanding to the many-sided challenge of the present crisis. He believes that the American people have the necessary wisdom and virtue to define their national interests in terms broad enough to take into account the legitimate interests and rights of other nations.

This brand of realism contributes to political insight and moral understanding because it helps to define the realm of what is humanly possible, the realm in which all moral and political judgments must be made. Religious ethics and politics are joined not in the pious platitudes of preachers and politicians, but in the real world of political decision. Christian ethics are concerned less with the projection of ideal goals for society than with the far more difficult problem of moving in the right direction with the highly rationed means available in the demanding arena of politics.

The essays in this volume deal with major facets of the international crisis during the past decade. Together they are a representative sample of Niebuhr's views, but they are only an introduction to the larger world of his political and religious thought.

Library of Congress

Washington, D. C.

Acknowledgments

The editor wishes to express special thanks to Professor Reinhold Niebuhr for his kind permission to reprint the essays in this volume and for his warm co-operation in the enterprise. He wishes also to thank the following publishers for permission to use essays which first appeared under their name: U.S. National Commission for UNESCO, Washington, D.C.; Charles Scribner's Sons, New York; *The New Leader*, New York; The Hazen Foundation, New Haven, Connecticut; *Foreign Affairs*, New York; and *Christianity and Crisis*, the journal edited by Professor Niebuhr and John C. Bennett.

The sources of the nine essays are listed on pages 127 and 128.

Contents

1. *The Challenge of the World Crisis*

If we are to gauge the available spiritual, moral, political and cultural resources of our nation, which are available for the performance of our responsibilities at this fateful juncture of world history, it is advisable to begin with an analysis of the dominant trends and forces of contemporary history, which have created the unique perils and opportunities confronting us. We may divide these forces and tendencies, complex as they are, chiefly into five great historical movements.

The first is the increasingly rapid growth of technics which has transmuted every international problem into a global one by confronting us with a potential global community or at least with a world-wide interdependence of the nations.

The second is derived from the first. It is the series of technical developments which have made wars lethal in that every conflict threatens to become an atomic one. Thus statecraft is confronted with a hazard which no previous statecraft has faced; for a mistake or miscalculation may result in a degree of disaster never before imagined or imaginable in history.

The third factor is a demonic politico-religious movement which has beguiled millions of people and made many nations captive by generating a political dynamic through a compound of utopian illusions and power impulses.

Fourth, while all these developments were taking place our nation rose to the dizzy eminence of being the most powerful among the nations of the "free" world.

Fifth, the contest between the free world and modern totalitarianism must be conducted at great hazard because of the vast social and political revolutions on the continents of Asia and Africa where hitherto subject peoples are either fighting for or celebrating their independence. They are animated by deep resentments against the imperialistic impact of a technically powerful Western culture upon the weaker nontechnical nations of Asia and Africa. The resentments were the more virulent because the "white man's arrogance" was compounded with the pride of power in this initial encounter.

We must consider more fully these five basic tendencies and forces in the contemporary situation before proceeding to an estimate of our resources for meeting our peculiar problems.

The Technical Revolution

The development of technics and the corresponding enlargement of the international community is of course not a recent development. The whole history of mankind has been influenced by the gradual development of technical competence both in the mastery of nature and in the arts of communication. But these developments proceeded by geometric progression in the latter half of the nineteenth century and the first half of the twentieth century. The airplane came into effective use in World War I and the jet airplane was developed in World War II. This development symbolized the increasing triumph of time over space in recent years and the consequent narrowing of the world's dimensions. The development of the radio in the same period also enhanced the contiguity of the national communities with each other.

Furthermore, world trade increasingly made the economic life of the nations mutually interdependent. Thus, in the period between the two world wars, the whole world suffered from a depression in its economic life. It is unnecessary to say that this greater intimacy and interdependence of the nations did not automatically create a world community for which the optimists of the previous century hoped. It created the possibility of such a community but also the possibility of enlarging every conflict between communities. In short, technical progress accentuated all problems of community and gave them new dimensions. We have to solve our international problems within the new dimensions established by an ever more successful technical civilization.

The Atomic Age

The second development is really a part of the first but it has such a significance that it deserves special mention. The development of nuclear physics and the consequent invention of atomic weapons of warfare are certainly an aspect of the triumph of technics. But there is a special significance in this development which prompts people to speak of our age as an "atomic age." The first bomb dropped on Japan was followed in quick succession by the report of the failure to outlaw atomic weapons through international action, the creation of bigger atom bombs, the report that Russia had learned how to make them, the development of the hydrogen bomb, and the subsequent report that Russia also was privy to this most dread of all secrets. This rapid succession of events was a clear indication of the speed at which modern history moves in all areas, but—ironically enough—particularly in the development of instruments of mutual annihilation. In less than a decade it became apparent that if another world war should occur it would be fought with weapons of such monstrous destructive power as to leave even the victor, in Mr. Churchill's phrase, an empty victory "in a universe of ruins." War meant mutual devastation in which the difference between victory and defeat might be slight indeed. Thus to all the dimensions of our contemporary international problems this dimension of possible mutual destruction was presented to a generation which had only recently dreamed of historical progress.

History is rather more unpredictable than we had imagined in past centuries and even in recent decades. Everyone thought that an armament race on the level of nuclear weapons would inevitably lead to war, even though such a war might mean mutual annihilation. But in recent years it has become apparent that the very hope-lessness of preventing any war from becoming an atomic one has become the only real source of hope that war may be prevented. Thus the dogma that armament races must inevitably lead to war has been challenged; and the hope of the scientist Nobel, the inventor of dynamite, that the destructiveness of modern weapons would prevent war, seems to have been belatedly justified after history seemed to make sport of such a hope for almost a century. At any rate, it is apparent that the present relaxation of tensions in the world is due to the realization on each side that any conflict might become one of global dimensions and that such a global struggle would also inevitably be an atomic war. Thus in Mr. Churchill's phrase "security has become the child of terror and survival the twin brother of annihilation."

International Communism

The third significant development of modern history which has accentuated what would in any case have been a very large problem of the integration of a potential world community is the growth of the most dynamic and demonic world politico-religious movement in history.

International communism has developed aspects both qualitatively and quantitatively that are among the most unpredicted forces in the contemporary scene. For the Communist movement has managed to compound power lusts with utopian dreams in such a way as to give its totalitarian practices a dynamism and a plausibility which no one could have foreseen in this age which prides itself on its enlightenment.

Communism is not a fortuitous corruption of the Marxist dogma, for its aberrations are directly derived from some of Marx's miscalculations in regard to the nature of man and human society. Its fury of self-righteousness and its vast monopolies of power against whose pretensions and aggressions there are no checks are directly derived from Marx's utopian vision of an innocent mankind, to be realized once the corruption due to the institution of property was removed. Yet Marx would probably have been horrified by the realities of the Communist empire and would also most probably have suffered the fate which the early Bolshevists suffered at the hands of Stalin in the purge trials of the thirties.

In short, the dream of the utopians of the past century turned into a nightmare of tyranny, not fortuitously, but also not by any conscious intent.

Fortunately the nations with a technical civilization were able to correct the injustices of their earlier industrialism and to perfect the balance of power in both their political and economic life to such a degree that they attained a measure of health which could serve as an antidote to the Communist poison. The false panacea generated in, and designed for, a technical society could find no foothold there. But it did find lodgement in the feudal-agrarian nations, first in Russia and then in China, so that communism dominates a great part of the world measured in either square miles of territory or in population.

It would be difficult to estimate the proportions of illusion and cynicism in the compound of motives that move the oligarchs of the present Communist imperium. They must know that the power realities do not conform to the original dream. But they may, for all we know, cling to shreds of the dream in order to validate their ambitions in their own minds and in those of their victims. They have at any rate enough remaining illusions to make their power very dangerous. In their eyes (at least until the atomic threat became serious) it was not necessary to concern themselves with the problem of mutual accommodation between foes or competitors or with that of integrating a divided world community, for they were privy to an historical logic which promised their cause victory over all its foes. These illusions even more than the unacknowledged power lusts impart a very dangerous irresponsibility to the foes of the free world and render the enmity which separates the Communist and the free world doubly dangerous.

The Communist danger is greater than the previous Nazi one for various reasons. According to the Stalinist revision of the Leninist revision of Marxism the first nation to have a successful revolution is in honor bound to come to the aid of still "enslaved proletarian" classes in the capitalist nations by military might and seek to "liberate" them. In short, no military venture is excluded from the strategy of communism. We have had several experiences with these military thrusts of the Communist power, most recently in Korea and in Indo-China. Nevertheless, communism does not, as did Nazism, rely primarily on military power. It is primarily a conspirational movement relying on infiltration and revolutionary strategies to accomplish its ends. Furthermore, it is not handicapped by the obvious nationalistic and racial pretensions of Nazism and is therefore not inhibited from posing as the "liberator" of "subject" nations in any part of the world. Russian nationalism or Chinese nationalism may be compounded with its universalistic pretensions, but this fact does not offer any initial hazard to its propaganda purposes. We are therefore confronted with a foe who can avail himself of every political as well as military weapon in the pursuit of his ends and who can obscure the unscrupulousness of his methods with idealistic pretensions. There has probably never been a more formidable and widespread political movement in all history than the movement with which we are confronted.

The Primacy of American Power

The fourth great historical movement that concerns us in describing our contemporary situation is the phenomenal rise of our own nation to the position of undisputed leadership in the world of free nations. This rise has been so phenomenal and rapid that one of our real problems as a nation is to become conscious of the degree of our power and of the responsibility which is the concomitant of power. Before the First World War we were content with our continental security and rather indifferent to the perils and opportunities of the world scene. We were also unconscious of the fact that a part of our security was not due to our continental isolation but was parasitic on the British navy. The whole international situation was economically and politically relatively stable because Britain, as the leading industrial nation and as the greatest naval power, "policed" the European world, or rather managed a precarious "balance of power." This relative peace was ended by the first German challenge to the whole equilibrium. The resulting war found us reluctant to participate in the hostilities though it soon became apparent that our national interests would be imperiled by a German victory. We entered the war peripherally and subsequent American policies seemed to make it very clear that we were determined never to enter another European war.

This determination showed that we were not aware either of the growth of our power or of the destruction of our continental security through the technical developments we have already discussed.

The second threat to the European community from a German tyranny proved to be both morally and politically more dangerous to us than the first one. But it did not immediately alter our fixed neutralist determination, which was embodied in much legislation designed to prevent our involvement in another war. Indeed we could probably not have followed the clear dictates of both our conscience and our national interests if Japan had not catapulted us into the war by her attack on Pearl Harbor.

The exertions of the war dissipated our neutralist illusions. When the war was over we emerged not only incomparably the most powerful of the free nations but committed to responsibilities commensurate with our power. The war did not suddenly increase our strength. On the contrary, our industrial production had been slowly increasing from 11 per cent of the world's industrial production in 1899 to 29 per cent in 1950. But the war did suddenly increase our military power and political prestige, chiefly because our economic plant was not impaired by the war and our productivity increased remarkably through the exertions of the war. In consequence, we proved at the end of the conflict to be the only nation with sufficient economic power to sustain the military force that was required to "police" the world and to help the impoverished economies of Europe so that they would not fall prey to the Communist virus.

Fortunately, immediate responsibilities proved to be more persuasive than abstract theorizing. Therefore the isolationist temper of the nation was dissipated completely and we moved from continental security to the position of the strongest nation in an alliance of free nations, forced to confront a world-wide Communist threat. History probably records no more rapid transformation of a national ethos than the one that was accomplished among us in the Second World War and the subsequent period. Nations which only yesterday feared or affected to fear our lack of a sense of continuing responsibility now have the contrary fear that we will not be flexible enough in leading the free world in its long exertions through a period of not so peaceful co-existence. We are not altogether persuaded of the genuineness of these fears, being suspicious that the envy of our fortune may predispose the nations poorer than we to engage in these critical judgments of our character. But in any case the rise of America to this position of world leadership has been phenomenal in both the rapidity of the development and degree of power and prestige which we have gained. It is one of the major factors in the contemporary world situation.

Revolutionary Ferments

The fifth development of which we must take account is the revolutionary ferments that are agitating the Asian and African continents, which complicate the encounter between the free world and communism. On these continents the nations are ethnically "colored." Their culture may be primitive or highly developed, but in any case their technical development has been retarded in comparison with the Western nations. Our contest with communism on these continents is complicated by three factors which must prove hazardous to any immediate success of our cause and which require a great deal of patience and expiation of past sins on our part.

First, there is the resentment felt by the colored peoples of the white man's long tradition of arrogance toward the peoples of darker pigment. This resentment is an embarrassment to our own nation particularly inasmuch as our past treatment of the Negroes, though rapidly changing, gives the Communist propaganda many targets for its arrows.

Second, resentment is felt by the "colonial" peoples against the initial impact of a technical civilization upon a nontechnical one. That first impact resulted in the application of the superior technical power of the Western nations for the purpose of bringing the nontechnical cultures into the orbit of the powerful nations either as the source of raw materials or as markets for new industrial enterprise. This "imperialism" was at times politically implemented and at times availed itself of economic means alone. In any case, it wounded the self-respect of the subject peoples and they feel and express their resentments even in a day when the weakening of the Western powers has led to the voluntary or forced emancipation of all the colonial peoples. These resentments are most sharp and vivid in the contemporary scene in such nations as Indo-China, where French imperialism beat such a tardy retreat that it played into the hands of the Communist aggressors.

Third, the present impact of a technical civilization upon these older organic cultures tends to destroy their organic forms and to render the feudal structure of their society morally and politically untenable. On the other hand, they can hardly acquire in a few decades the delicate balances of power in both the economic and political spheres by which democratic justice and liberty are achieved and which the Western nations required about four centuries to learn.

The disintegration of a feudal or even a tribal social order under the impact of modern technics coupled with the inability to create a democratic order in so short a time is the greatest of the hazards which the free world faces on the two continents in its contest with communism. A democratic political order resting on the "consent of the governed" requires a literate and intelligent electorate and some force of social cohesion strong enough to permit the stresses and strains of democratic diversity of opinion. In Western history the "middle class" of professional and business people, who are not economically dependent upon a "lord," were the primary agents of this political development. But justice in a technical society requires not only a broad base of political power, inherent in universal suffrage; it requires also balances of power in the economic sphere, such as developed in the trade union movement in Western society. Without such balances the centralization of power in industrialism may, as in our earlier industrial history, aggravate the injustices of the traditional society and create the resentments and confusions upon which communism feeds. It must be remembered that the recently emancipated nations are subject to the very conditions which gave the Marxist dogma its plausibility in nineteenth century Europe, and which occasioned some of the earlier Communist triumphs in Europe before a viable justice under conditions of freedom made the European community essentially immune to the Communist virus.

For these reasons we must expect some initial defeats on these continents as we have experienced them in China and Indo-China. We must not expect these recently emancipated peoples, much as they enjoy their collective freedom from imperialism, either to value, or to be competent in manipulating, the civil freedom of an open society. They may therefore move from the collectivism of an organic society to modern totalitarianism without being aware of the danger in this new collectivism. They may fancy that there is a greater affinity between communism and the old society than between the old organic communities and the complex realities of the political and economic life in modern democracies. This gives communism an initial advantage over us even though history proves the new collectivism to be a grievous tyranny, which makes the old imperialism seem benign by comparison.

In nations like India which have had some experience with democracy but which harbor many resentments against past subjection, a neutralist reaction to the conflict between Western democracy and communism is a rather natural, if not an inevitable, policy.

The Resulting Challenge

If we summarize the contemporary situation which our nation faces we can succinctly express our dilemma in this way: We have been called into leadership of the free nations at the moment in history in which a potential world community is forming but has not yet been actualized. Every problem of the world community is aggravated by the world-wide influences of the Communist movement, having its power center in Russia but possessing tremendous influence throughout the world and availing itself of every conspiratorial, as well as military, weapon to enhance its power. We must wrestle with this dangerous foe with courage but also with caution because there is always the danger that local conflicts may become global and that any such war will become an atomic one with mutual annihilation as a possible consequence.

We have this position of leadership in the free world chiefly by reason of our tremendous economic power and our consequent military might. We must exercise our leadership of the free world in the light of tremendous complications in our contest with communism because the Asian and African continents are in ferment. Nationalistic ambitions and resentments because of previous subjection and the decay of agrarian social orders under the impact of technics all combine to make for political creativity, but also for confusion. They offer communism precisely the initial toehold which it briefly had in Western civilization and which a greater measure of justice in our political and economic life tended to overcome. It will be recognized that this complex of historical conditions, including the brevity of our apprenticeship in world leadership and the swiftness of our rise to power, presents our nation with the most exacting challenge in our history and one more exacting than faced by any other nation in world history.

2. America's Moral and Spiritual Resources

The moral and spiritual resources of the United States flow from three streams in our national heritage: (a) the traditions of our history which do much to determine our behavior even as individuals are influenced by their own peculiar history; (b) the religious traditions which inform the cultural life of our nation and set the ultimate standards upon the basis of which we make our immediate decisions; (c) the sum total of our cultural and scientific disciplines which enable us to weigh and gauge all the political, social, and moral factors which enter into our situation.

We must not define our "spiritual" resources too narrowly in traditional religious terms. We cannot forget that the very creation of our free society was the joint achievement of religious and "secular" forces.

The religious heritage supplied the realism which distrusted sinful man to such a degree that no position of power in the community was allowed to remain unchecked or unchallenged. The distinguishing mark of Anglo-Saxon democracy is precisely the rigor with which even the power of majorities is checked in the interest of minorities, and every kind of political power is made responsible. It can be safely said that this was the achievement of Christian radicalism as compared with the more rationalistic utopian radicalism of France. In our own country this realism was introduced particularly by the author of our Constitution, James Madison. Without this realism the democracy of France soon degenerated into Jacobin fanaticism and ultimately to Bonapartist absolutism. The religious forces rooted in the biblical faith also provided the ultimate and transcendent point of reference for the meaning of human existence, the faith in God which enabled men to say courageously, "We must obey God rather than men," to any community or any tyrant that tried to subject all human purposes to a social or political process. It gave man as a "child of God" the dignity to resist the fate of being merely an instrument of a process. This "dignity" was emphasized very much in all modern democratic theories, but the theories frequently outraged the very dignity which they affirmed.

In addition to the religious and spiritual resources of our historic faiths, we can without vainglory point to a unique aspect of American life which may be a resource to us now. This is our ethnic, cultural, and religious pluralism and the comparative absence of resentment among the various religious groups. This lack of resentment is probably due to the fact that no group has official preference among us. At any rate even our European critics give us credit for the virtue of tolerance. Our pluralistic society may help us in coming to terms with the inevitably pluralistic world society.

On the other hand, the secular disciplines, frequently so defective in their ultimate frame of reference, nevertheless provided the discriminating judgments which made it possible for modern men to analyze the complex problems of economic and political justice and to puncture the pretensions of religious people who sought to make religious faith an instrument of political power.

If we define the sources of our capacities for dealing with our international problems so as to include both our religious heritage and our secular disciplines we shall discover the relevance of this distinction in almost every area of application which we must now examine in detail. We shall note three major areas of application.

Realism Without Cynicism

First, we must develop a realism without cynicism which knows how to come to terms with the Communist menace on every level where it is a danger to the world. Communism faces us as a military power and as a political force which uses every form of resentment and discontent as grist for its revolutionary mills. A realistic defense against communism must not be indifferent to the military threat, but must also avoid a too great emphasis on military power alone. Mr. Churchill has given it as his opinion that our superiority in atomic weapons is the chief factor in our security; and he is probably right. He also expressed the opinion that the superiority would last not much more than four years. Yet, as we noted earlier, there is now an obvious relaxation of tensions which leads to the conviction that our security is established partly by our superiority in atomic weapons and partly by the fear on both sides of the consequences of an atomic war.

There is an ironic element in this development. We are now in the possession of the ultimate in weapons of warfare. Yet only a few decades ago a large section of our religious community was fearful of our involvement in any military encounter on the ground that such encounter would rob us of our innocency as a nation. The development of atomic weapons to the point of the hydrogen bomb for the sake of exercising our responsibilities toward the free world is the measure of our growing political and moral maturity. We now know that we cannot be responsible without guilt. For all responsibility is exercised in a field where partial and fragmentary values are supported against contending forces, and the ultimate exercise of responsibility may involve the guilt of the destruction of life. We must be realistic enough to guard our liberties against any use of force by the foe.

But now, only a few decades after we were exercised about the use of any military weapons at all, we are under the opposite danger of relying too exclusively upon these weapons in general, and on atomic weapons in particular. A word must be said about each one of these temptations in turn.

A too heavy reliance on atomic weapons may be caused by the cheapness of these weapons in comparison with conventional military equipment. Considerations of economy and a balanced budget might cause us to neglect standard military strength, including the infantry. But this kind of strategy would make us weak in a local encounter with the foe, such as we had in Korea, and would therefore increase the danger of a local conflict becoming a global one. One of the reasons for the opposition of some of the best nuclear physicists to the development of the hydrogen bomb was the fear of such a disproportion in our defense strategy.

The greater danger is that we will rely too much on military strength in general and neglect all the other political, economic, and moral factors which give unity, health, and strength to the nations of the free world. We are tempted to this false strategy by some interesting facets of our growth into a world power. We have previously observed that this growth was very rapid. This rapidity, combined with our lack of experience as an "imperial" power, made it difficult for us to gauge and appreciate the factors of prestige and traditional loyalty, of ethnic and linguistic sources of political cohesion, and all the complex political factors that enter into the forming of community and the acquisition of prestige and authority in the community, whether national or international.

Patience and Courage

A second major requirement is to develop patience and courage to outlast a tenacious foe in a long struggle in which the issue can never be allowed to come to a final arbitrament. Of all the tests upon our leadership this is probably the most difficult one. There are elements in our national history that make it very hard for us to pass this test.

Compared with other nations we have had a very brief history and during our short span of existence we have suffered no serious defeats, nor have we been subject to the kind of frustration that we now experience in our contest with communism, in which it is impossible to come to a clear-cut issue with the foe without involving ourselves and the world in catastrophe. It is very difficult for a young and vigorous nation lacking the experience of frustration, to cope with the situation in which we are now involved. Our resulting impatience is aggravated by certain notes in the secular portion of our culture. These are derived from the notion that the mastery of historical destiny waits only upon the proper scientific technics, and is not essentially different from the mastery of nature. The historical situation we now face, in which there can be no immediate or clear-cut victory for our cause nor any release for decades from the burdens and anxieties which we must bear, is therefore not according to the experiences of a youthful nation nor according to the hopes of a secular culture.

In this situation we must draw upon the resources of our religious heritage. For the biblical faiths of our three major religious traditions have a clear knowledge of the fact that men and nations, however powerful they are, can never unambiguously master their fate. It is the fate of man, according to these faiths, that he always remain a *creative creature* and therefore both creature and creator of the historical process. This conception implies that men's and nation's ambitions are naturally subject to frustration, that human ends can never be satisfied precisely as men intend. The frustrations that we face as a nation may not have been foreseen according to our national experience but they are anticipated in the great faiths which look upon the human situation from within a frame of meaning which endows human history with significance but according to which all fulfillments of meaning are fragmentary and all meanings are themselves partially obscured. History, in short, points beyond itself for its fulfillment. It is one of the causes of the Communist evil that it is a secular faith which tries to complete history within itself. This utopianism becomes very dangerous when it is made the basis of a political program.

Men and nations are as far from omniscience

as from omnipotence. A wise statecraft tries to foresee as much of the future as possible but it is also conscious of the limits of man's foreknowledge. The biblical maxim, "Sufficient unto the day is the evil thereof," is therefore an expression of true statesmanship. Such a maxim precludes strategies like "preventive" war. For all such strategies seek to prevent what is regarded as a clear future danger by resolute immediate action.

Mutuality with Allies

Third, we must summon our resources, both religious and secular, for the purpose of establishing real mutuality between ourselves and our allies, despite the great disparity of power and fortune between us. The task of relating our nation mutually to an alliance of free nations has two dimensions. The one would have existed even if our nation were not so powerful and fortunate. The other is given by the unique facts of our common life with other nations. This uniqueness is determined by the phenomenal dimension of the American power and prosperity in comparison with the poorer and weaker nations of Europe and of Asia.

Even if our nation were not so powerful we

should find it as difficult as do other nations to be interested in the welfare of the peoples beyond our national borders. The power of collective self-concern is older than America. The nation as the most powerful community and therefore as the most potent bearer of this collective self-interest, is a comparatively recent development, but it is older than our own country. For the national community emerged from the disintegration of the medieval system of society and has been potent ever since. The power of collective self-interest presents us with a moral and political problem of great magnitude. It is not easy for a nation to be concerned with any other nation in altruistic terms.

The difference between individual and collective morality is immense and is established by the fact that collective self-concern is a compound of individual egotism, collectively expressed, and the spirit of loyalty and self-sacrifice of the individual which the community easily appropriates for its own ends. It was a dictum of George Washington that a nation was not to be trusted beyond its own interests; and on the whole this realistic advice has been the guide of all political science. But a mere consideration of the power of concern for the national interest easily obscures another side of the equation, namely, that self-concern can be as self-defeating in collective as in individual behavior. Nations as well as individuals stand under the law: "Whosoever seeketh to gain his life will lose it." In more concrete terms this means that a nation that is too preoccupied with its own interests is bound to define those interests too narrowly. It will do this because it will fail to consider those of its interests which are *bound up in a web of mutual interests* with other nations.

In short, the national interest when conceived only from the standpoint of the self-interest of the nation is bound to be defined too narrowly and therefore to be self-defeating. In both our secular and religious traditions there have been morally idealistic emphases which have recognized this aspect of man's collective life and have sometimes gone so far as to define patriotism as a form of treason to the larger community. But this form of idealism was usually blind to the persistence of the factor of collective self-regard and to the impossibility of either suppressing it completely or of transmuting it. On the other hand, the "realist" reaction to what was regarded as sentimentality was usually blind to the self-defeating nature of pure self-regard. We must draw on the profounder sources in our religious tradition and of our secular disciplines to solve this problem.

There are two aspects in a tolerable solution. First, we must realize that it is not within the realm of moral possibilities to ask a nation to be "self-sacrificing." There are various reasons for this, including the fact that the government which sacrifices the interests of a nation for the "common good" is in a very different situation from that of the individual who may decide to subordinate or sacrifice his own interests for a higher value. The art of statecraft is to find the point of concurrence between the parochial and the general interest, between the national and the international common good. It does not occur to any statesman to define a desired policy in any other term but that of such concurrence; and to justify it in terms of "wise self-interest." Moralists sometimes suggest that this establishes a too sharp distinction between individual and collective morality; but it must be observed that a free society in contrast to a tyrannical one, seeks to harness rather than to suppress particular individual interests in establishing the common good. In our immediate situation this policy means that we must try to persuade the nation that what is good for the alliance of the free nations is good for our own nation *in the long run*. A prudent self-regard must obviously prefer long-run to short-run ends because there are too many conflicts of interest in the short run between the particular and the general interest.

But this "realist" approach to the problem of national morality is obviously defective, even if prudence insists on the long run rather than the short run in calculating the concurrence of interests. The defect arises from the fact that any kind of prudence which estimates common problems from the perspective of a particular interest will define the interest too narrowly. It is necessary, therefore, to draw upon another moral and spiritual resource to widen the conception of interest. The citizens of a nation must have loyalties and responsibilities to a wider system of values than that of the national interest—to a civilization for instance, to a system of justice, and to a community of free nations. These moral concerns will serve to leaven the mind of a nation and prevent a national community from defining its interest too narrowly. The sense of justice must prevent prudence from becoming too prudential in defining interest. Such a combination of "idealism" and "realism" is given in

the great historic faiths. Without the insights of
these faiths, realism may degenerate into cynicism and idealism into sentimentality. They may
even degenerate within the context of these
faiths. But ideally the presuppositions of biblical
faiths insist on both the moral imperative of the
love commandment and the fact of the persistence of self-love in actual history. There is in
these faiths therefore a safeguard against both
sentimentality and moral cynicism. This must
be made available to the nation in the present
period of critical decisions in which we cannot
afford to disregard either the moral possibilities
or the moral realities of our common life.

The general problem of mutuality between
nations is aggravated in our case by the special
circumstances that our nation is very fortunate
and very powerful in comparison with the nations
allied with us. This disparity places a special
strain on mutuality and offers us special temptations to vanity and arrogance which militate
against our moral prestige and authority. It also
offers the other nations temptation to envy and
resentment against our power and fortune—a
temptation that would be present even if our
policies were always exemplary. Our power is
of course not solely a hazard to the mutuality of

the nations in our alliance. It is also creative because it furnishes the nucleus of undisputed authority which is so necessary for the integration of an alliance, particularly one which still lacks sufficient constitutional instruments of cohesion. Our undisputed power, whether wielded wisely or not, is certainly more conducive to unity than would be the divided power of two equally strong nations. The disintegration of the Delian League in the days of the rivalry for hegemony between Athens and Sparta, is an interesting lesson in history of the perils to unity in such rivalries. But the creative aspects of the hegemony of our nation must not blind us to the perils which inhere in the phenomenal superiority of our power and wealth. Every moral, cultural, and spiritual resource must be summoned to make such power sufferable to our allies and to ourselves.

The first resource must be a frame of meaning for the historical drama in which we are involved, one that will set the power of our nation in proper perspective and prevent the individual citizen from viewing the nation and its power idolatrously as the source and end of his existence, and will guard against the arrogance and vainglory in which all powerful nations are tempted to indulge. We who are adherents of the great historic faiths believe that faith in a sovereign God "who bringeth princes to naught and maketh the judges of the earth as vanity," in a God whose majesty dwarfs the majesty of even the most powerful nation, is such a resource. The most perennial heresy in the life of mankind is the worship of the nation as if it were God. The empires of ancient history—Egypt, Babylon and Rome—frankly constructed religions which sanctified this false frame of meaning.

It is not possible to do this explicitly in the framework of religions which acknowledge a divine sovereignty that is not dependent upon the pride and power of nations. But we must humbly acknowledge that nationalistic arrogance and vainglory have been expressed within the framework of the Christian and Jewish faiths. Therefore we cannot declare that even a valid religious faith, which does not identify God with the Nation, is perfect proof against such arrogance. Therefore we need another resource beside the obviously religious one. That resource is furnished by every discipline which puts us in touch with the world, showing the effects of our policies upon other people and nations upon whom our power impinges.

It is necessary, for instance, to have a clear view of the British attitude toward our policies.

Britain not only has accumulated experience and wisdom in foreign relations, which we must share as we did in fact share them in our yielding to the British insistence that there be a conference with Russia "at the summit." Britain is also the dominant power most clearly displaced by the rapid development of our hegemony. There are therefore bound to be some resentments against us in Britain, though it is significant that these resentments are more moderate than those in other, less powerful nations. We must know how our power impinges upon France—and incidentally moderate our impatience with French resentments. They are probably more virulent than those of any other nation because France is a deeply frustrated nation. It has won a war but is in the process of losing its empire after spending much blood and treasure to save it. The losses were undoubtedly due to the French tardiness in granting its colonial peoples genuine independence. But dwelling on this is not helpful now.

The Discipline of Religion

We live by a religious faith which affirms that "a man's life consisteth not in the abundance of the things which he possesseth." Such a faith pressed too consistently may lead to an ascetic life denial or at least to a denial of the ordinary comforts of life. But it may be questioned whether our culture has not lost that essential religious reservation about the *goals* of life which prevent a too great preoccupation with the *goods* of life. It is difficult to see how this trend in our culture can be reversed even by the most potent religious revival; and it is equally questionable whether such a reversal would be serviceable either to ourselves or to the world at this juncture of history. It must be remembered that most of our critics would like to have some of the comforts and dimensions of natural well-being for which they criticize us!

It is probably idle to hope for the reversal of so strong a cultural trend as our preoccupation with technics. The best we can hope for is that the wealth so acquired will be dedicated to the task of giving strength to the free community of nations. If we could say, "God be thanked who matched us with this hour"; if we could be thrilled with our historic opportunities and cease to regret our burdens as involving high taxes; and if we could realize that our burdens are an opportunity to make our wealth sufferable to our conscience and tolerable to our friends—then we would redeem even that part of our culture which our critics may deem least honorable.

"A Moment to Decide"

We are living in a grand and awful period of history in which every illusion, nourished in past centuries, has brought forth its evil fruits; in which every new power developed by man, particularly in his conquest of nature, reveals its capacity for both good and evil; and in which the highest possibilities are inextricably intermingled with the most dire perils.

There are no certain climaxes of history since every conceivable climax may, for all we know, be succeeded by a more vivid one. But compared with the past we are certainly living in the most impressive climax of history, judged both quantitatively and qualitatively. Our nation has been destined to play a very responsible role in this climax. Our decisions can become fateful for the very survival of our civilization. In this historical context, it is important to draw upon every resource in our several faiths, in our tradition, and in our immediate vitalities so that we shall not "meanly lose but nobly save the last best hope of earth."

3. Why Is Communism So Evil?*

What makes communism so evil and what are the sources of its malignancy? We are bound to ask the question because we are fated as a generation to live in the insecurity which this universal evil of communism creates for our world. The timid spirits ask another question: is communism really as evil as we now think; or are we tempted by the tensions of our conflict with it to exaggerate our negative judgments about it, somewhat as we did in judging the Kaiser's Germany, which we erroneously regarded as about as evil as Hitler's Germany subsequently proved to be.

It is important to analyze the nature of the Communist evil—both for the sake of those who take its evil for granted but do not bother to diagnose its nature or trace its sources; and for

49

the sake of those deluded spirits who imagine that communism is but a different version of a common democratic creed, a difference which might be resolved if a dissipation of the war psychosis would permit us to engage in the enterprise. We must analyze it too for the sake of those who assess the degree of evil in communism correctly but prove their confusion in regard to its nature by comparing it with something much less evil than itself, as for instance the former State Department official who asserted that communism was "nothing but" the old Russian imperialism in a new form. This judgment obscured the difference between the comparatively ordinate and normal lust for power of a great traditional nation and the noxious demonry of this world-wide secular religion.

If we seek to isolate the various causes of an organized evil which spreads terror and cruelty throughout the world and confronts us everywhere with faceless men who are immune to every form of moral and political suasion, we must inevitably begin with the monopoly of power which communism establishes. Disproportions of power anywhere in the human community are fruitful of injustice, but a system which gives some men absolute power over other men results in evils which are worse than injustice. Evidence drawn from the records of armies of occupation throughout history proves the deleterious effect of absolute power, impinging upon powerlessness, on both those who have power and those who lack it.

We must draw a distinction between the theory which makes for a monopoly of power and the practical effects of such a monopoly. Socialists may, for instance, share a similar theory with communism; but, though they are inserted into the wholesome balances of power of a democracy, their actions and character are different from those of the Communist oligarchs. On the other hand, socialists are wrong if they interpret present Communist practices as merely the fortuitous corruption of the original Marxist ideals. Marxism did not indeed plan the highly centralized power structure of communism; but Marx did plan for a "dictatorship of the proletariat"; and the progressive moral deterioration of such a dictatorship was inevitable rather than fortuitous, for two reasons: The first is that when society is divided into the powerful and the powerless there is no way of preventing the gradual centralization of the monopoly of power. The monopoly of a class becomes the monopoly

of the party which claims to be the vanguard of
the whole class; the monopoly of the party gradually becomes the monopoly of a small oligarchy
who speak at first for the class to other classes
who have been robbed of power. But their
authority inevitably degenerates into a monopoly
of power exercised over their own party and class
because no one in the whole community has the
constitutional means to challenge and check
the inevitable extension of power after which
the most powerful grasp. The dictatorship of the
oligarchy further degenerates into the dictatorship of a single tyrant. It was significant that a
fallen oligarch, such as Trotsky, was as powerless
as the most powerless peasant to challenge the
rule of the tyrant who had defeated him, or to
amend the history of the events written by the
victor to justify his victory and to discredit his
foe.

Another reason for the excessive concentration
of power is that the Marxist theory wrongly
assumes that economic power inheres solely in
the ownership of property and obscures the
power of the manager of property. It therefore
wrongly concludes that the socialization of property causes economic power to evaporate when
in fact it merely gives a single oligarchy a

monopoly of both economic and political power. One pathetic consequence of this error is that the workers of a socialized concern, who are in theory the common owners of the property and are therefore prevented from holding any significant power, are rendered powerless against the managerial oligarchs who run the factory. The inevitable result is the accumulation of injustices more grievous than those which originally inspired the Marxist revolt against a free society.

While the relation of absolute power to complete defenselessness is the basic cause of all the evils of communism, it must be recognized that the Communist tyranny is supported and aggravated by the whole series of pretensions derived from the secular religion which creates the ethos of the Communist society. The most significant moral pretension is derived from the utopian illusions of Marxism. According to these illusions every policy of Marxist propaganda and class conflict has the object of hastening the day of historical climax when an ideal classless society will emerge. The utopian illusions presumably make communism more dangerous rather than more evil. They are responsible for the loyalty of a group of intellectuals to the Communist cause. The disillusionment of these idealists in

Europe does not prevent a new crop of Asian intellectuals from being taken in by these pretensions. Furthermore, the illusions enable Communists to pose as the liberators of every class or nation which they intend to enslave; and to exploit every moral and political weakness of the civilized world as if they had the conscience of civilization in their keeping.

The utopian illusions undoubtedly make communism more dangerous than Nazism, which could not, for instance, have conquered either Poland or China by internal conspiracy. The power of the illusions is proved by the fact that the most consistent foes of communism feel themselves compelled to argue that it is as bad as Nazism, contending that the tyrannical practice is the same whatever the contradiction between the different theories of moral cynicism and utopianism which inspire them. These arguments imply that there is a virtue in the utopian ideal which the practice unfortunately belies. The fact is that the utopianism is the basis of the evil in communism as well as of its greater danger. It provides a moral façade for the most unscrupulous political policy, giving the Communist oligarch the moral warrant to suppress and sacrifice immediate values in the historical process for the sake of reaching so ideal a goal. It may be unfair to compare the strain of utopianism in our liberal culture with the Communist utopianism. But it is not unfair to suggest that the attractive power of communism for many so-called idealists is due to a general utopian element in our culture which fails to acknowledge the perennial moral contradictions on every level of historical advance.

We cannot suppose that the ruthless oligarchs in the Kremlin exercise their power without a measure of cynicism; but such are the powers of human self-deception that for all we know, they may still be believers who persuade themselves that they are doing what they do for noble ultimate ends. Stalin is reported to have rebuffed a journalist who compared him with Napoleon. Napoleon, he declared, had no good purpose as the goal for which his power was the means. In one sense the presence or absence of cynicism among the oligarchs is beside the point. The important point is that the ruthless power operates behind a screen of pretended ideal ends, a situation which is both more dangerous and more evil than pure cynical defiance of moral ends. It corresponds to the weakness of the human heart more nearly than absolute cynicism, for men are less inclined to pure cynicism than to the delusion that they serve some noble purpose in engaging in projects which serve their own end.

The fierce self-righteousness derived from these utopian illusions is accentuated by the Marxist distinction between the classes, according to which the classes which hold property are naturally evil while the "proletariat," the industrial workers, are the Messianic class endowed with every virtue. A derivative of this distinction distinguishes between the capitalist nations which are by nature "imperialistic" and "militaristic" and the innocent "Peoples' Democracies." The tendency to call white black and black white is accentuated and justified by these unreal distinctions. The fury of Communist self-righteousness is aggravated furthermore by the Marxist error of equating egotism with the economic motive so that the most powerful oligarch, driven and corrupted by the lust for power, will appear innocent to his own conscience and the delusions of his community because he makes no profit and owns no property.

A third pretension of communism is usually obscured by the stock criticism against Marxism. It is rightly accused of being deterministic, that

is, of underestimating the freedom of man and
of emphasizing the determined character of his
culture and of his convictions, which are said
to be rooted in his economic interest. This de-
terminism is at least half true and not nearly so
dangerous as a supplementary and contradictory
dogma according to which history works toward
a climax in which the proletarian class must, by
a "revolutionary act," intervene in the course of
history and thereby change not only history but
the whole human situation; for after this act
man is no longer both creature and creator of
history but purely the creator who "not only
proposes but also disposes." This idea involves
monstrous claims of both omnipotence and omniscience which support the actual monopoly of
power and aggravate its evil. Molotov illustrates
the pretensions of omniscience when he declares
that the Communists, guided by "Marxist-
Leninist science," know not only the inner meaning of current events but are able to penetrate
the curtain of the future and anticipate its events.
This tendency of playing God to human history
is the cause for a great deal of Communist
malignancy. The seemingly opposite tendency
to regard men as the product of economic cir-
cumstance supports the pretension; for it makes

it possible for a group of elite to pretend to be the manipulators of the destiny of their fellow men. The pretension reveals the similarity between the Nazi evil, based upon the pretensions of Nietzsche's "superman," who makes his power self-justifying, and this kind of superman whose power is ostensibly justified by the fate which appoints him as the creator of historical destiny. Some of the Communist fury is the consequence of the frustration of the Communist oligarchs, when they discover history to be more complex than anticipated in their logic and find that opposing forces which are marked for defeat in their apocalypse, show a more stubborn strength and resistance than they anticipated.

The Marxist dogmatism, coupled with its pretensions of scientific rationality, is an additional source of evil. The dogmas are the more questionable because the tyrannical organization prevents a re-examination of the dogmas when the facts refute them. Ideally, the presuppositions which govern an inquiry into the facts are more inescapable than a liberal culture supposes. It ostensibly believes in the possibility of empirical inquiry without presuppositions, though it has its own dogmas of the idea of progress and the perfectibility of man, for instance; but it is im-

portant to have the freedom to re-examine and
to dismiss a presupposition if it is refuted by
history. The Communist irrationality and dogmatism consists of a rigorous adherence to
dogma in defiance of the facts. In this it differs
from Nazi irrationality which relies upon mystic
intuitions. The Communists test every historical
fact with ostensible precision and coolness, but
their so-called science looks at the world through
the spectacles of inflexible dogma which alters
all the facts and creates a confused world picture. The greatest danger of Communist policy
comes from the fact that the Communists do not
know what kind of world they live in, and what
their foes are like. Their own rigorous dogma
obscures the facts and their tyrannical system
prevents, for motives of fear, the various pro-
consuls of their imperium from apprising the
men in the Kremlin of the truth.

The rigor of the Communist dogmatism
creates an idealogical inflexibility, consonant
with the monolithic political structure. Sig-
nificantly the hope inside and outside the party
that Communist inflexibility would be modified,
for instance, by the Western traditions of Czech-
oslovakia or the Confucian traditions of China,
proved to be mistaken. Communism has been

consistently totalitarian in every political and historical environment. Nothing modifies its evil display of tyranny. The combination of dogmatism and tyranny leads to shocking irrationalities in Communist trials, where the victims are made to confess to the most implausible charges. Since the Communist dogma allows for no differences of opinion among the elect, every deviation from orthodoxy is not only branded as treason, but is attributed to some original sinful social taint. Thus the fallen Czech Communist leader Slansky confesses that his alleged "nationalist-Zionist" treason must be attributed to his "bourgeois-nationalist" origin.

It is instructive that the actual monopoly of power accentuates the evil in the ideological pretensions of communism while these pretensions give a spiritual dimension to the evils which flow from a monopoly of power. Thus the evil of communism flows from a combination of political and "spiritual" factors, which prove that the combination of power and pride is responsible for turning the illusory dreams of yesterday into the present nightmare that disturbs the ease of millions of men in our generation.

4. *The Anatomy of American Nationalism*

Our nationalist circles, chiefly in the right wing of the Republican party, have had a pronounced preference for Asia, rather than Europe, in our over-all strategy against communism. This preference has been persistent and consistent. In World War II, the nationalists insisted that we defeat Japan before we tackled the more formidable Nazi foe. Since then, they have believed that we lost China merely by false decisions in the State Department, particularly by giving the Chinese Nationalists too grudging and tardy support. They think that we could have settled scores in Asia if MacArthur had been given a free hand.

This curious preference for Asia leaves the political and moral factors out of account. It derives from blindness to the fact that in Asia we meet the Communist foe across the vast expanse of a disintegrating colonialism and decaying feudalism. We are at a disadvantage because the former colonial peoples are filled with resentment against the first imperial impact of a Western technical civilization upon the agrarian and, incidentally, "colored" world; because Asia does not prize the liberties of a democratic political order which has slowly developed in a technical civilization, and is always tempted to exchange the injustices of its decaying feudalism and the inequalities of its recent colonialism for the brutalities of a technically equipped despotism.

Our nationalists are equally oblivious to the fact that in Europe we are defending the technical power of the West and that we are bound to the European nations by centuries of common cultural and political inheritance. Any tendency to go farther in Asian military ventures than our European allies think prudent from the standpoint both of their own interests and of the success of our common cause, runs the danger of involving us in a full-scale war without the support of our Western allies.

Why should our nationalists persist in strategies which imperil our leadership of the free world and complicate the task of beating communism in the long trial of competitive co-existence? The question is partly answered by the Formosa crisis of early 1955 and MacArthur's

speech in Los Angeles. In both cases, the causes
of this nationalist orientation are seen to be an
undue reliance on purely military power (with
a concomitant blindness to the political and
moral factors) and an almost pathological impatience with the frustrations of forces beyond
our control, which are new to a nation so suddenly vaulted into Western leadership.

Formosa undoubtedly has some strategic importance, and we are right to exert our power
in holding it against the Communists. The British
Government's support of our Formosa policy,
despite strong Labor opposition, proves that this
fact is appreciated in Europe. But the emotional
capital invested by Americans in Formosa stems
not from strategic considerations but from the
idea that the Chinese Nationalists might have
been successful had we given them full support.
(Incidentally, one hears less and less from our
nationalists about unleashing the Chinese Nationalists against the mainland; it has become
apparent that they could not succeed without
our total involvement.) The fact that the British
and other Europeans are not too critical of our
Formosa policy can be understood only on the
basis of their recognition that the defense of
Formosa means also "leashing" the Nationalist

forces against any mainland adventure. They regard our policy in other words, as the best possible means of liquidating the political heritage in China, a heritage occasioned by the illusion that there was a purely military answer to the Asian problem.

General MacArthur's birthday address in Los Angeles sheds even more light on the nationalist motivation. MacArthur clearly is bewildered by the historical frustrations to which this nation is subject. "We are told," he declared, "that we must go on indefinitely as at present. Some say fifty years or more. What is the end? None say. There is no definite objective. We must pass on to those who follow us the search for a final solution."

This situation is clearly intolerable to a man who defines the young in heart as those who seek for victory. The inconclusiveness of history is not regarded by MacArthur as one of its inescapable characteristics, but as the consequence of false doctrine. He is on this point the spokesman of those in our nation who are unable to comprehend why we had more control over our destiny in the days of our infancy than in the day of our maturity and seeming omnipotence. The obvious cause of this paradox is that we are enmeshed in a skein of history which dwarfs even our great power and leaves us with no alternative to a patient and courageous waiting upon the tortuous processes of history, which may solve some problems that the mere exertion of our power cannot solve.

MacArthur's second thesis is even more revealing. "The military situation," he declared, "demonstrates the inherent weakness of a system of collective security. The chain is no stronger than its weakest link. What is even more vital, the full power can be brought into action only when all the links function simultaneously. But this is difficult, since the diverse interests of the allies tend to separation rather than unity."

Here is the clue to our impatience with Europe. It is the continent of our allies, who are tardy or recalcitrant about any given policy of ours. Asia, on the other hand, is a continent of many millions of square miles and hundreds of millions of population, in which we could vanquish the enemy if only we could give full play to our military power. The fact that we are at a great moral and political disadvantage on this continent does not occur to our nationalists, because, in their political immaturity, they are able to measure only the ponderables of military power and not the imponderables of the political order. Admiral Radford has probably never given serious thought to the problem of fighting communism on the political and moral level in Asia and encountering both justified and unjustified resentments, as well as utopian illusions, in this moral encounter.

General MacArthur does not follow the logic of most of the nationalists, however. He expresses their impatience with political frustration and with any system of collective security. Logically, this would force him to counsel unleashing American military power without hindrance from any inconvenient ally. That seems to be the spoken and unspoken policy of the American nationalists. For some reason, perhaps because a modicum of military realism lingers in the mind of the great general, MacArthur takes a quite different, though equally irrelevant, tack. He comes to the conclusion that in this situation nothing but the abolition of war will solve our problems.

"Whatever betides," he said at Los Angeles, "the fate of the Far East, or indeed of the world, will not be settled by force of arms. We may all be annihilated, but war cannot be the arbiter of our survival." MacArthur does not suggest the practical steps which must be taken in the present situation to accomplish the abolition of war, though he hints that if modern statesmen had ordinary intelligence, they would soon attain this desirable goal. This breath-taking retreat to an impossible "idealism" from an equally impossible "realism" makes MacArthur's thoughts irrelevant to the anxious citizens of this generation.

The alternation between equally irrelevant forms of idealism and realism may be "typically American" in a sense. We are a politically adolescent nation, not fully accustomed to the responsibilities and perplexities of maturity. And so we may alternate between the temptation to "take arms against a sea of troubles," using our strength to resolve all perplexities, and the temptation to flee into an illusory heaven of innocence from the hard realities of our life. It must be said in MacArthur's favor that the inconsistent pacifism which crowns his thought is not so dangerous as the more consistent isolationist nationalism of the rest of his crew who proclaim him a hero.

Fortunately, this nationalism, based upon a too-simple reliance upon our military power and an understandable, though dangerous, impatience with historical frustrations, is not a general phenomenon in our nation. The common people and many of their leaders are quite aware of the perils in which we live as a nation and as a civilization. They know, too, that there are no swords of power to cut the Gordian knot of our history. One of the chief strands in this knot is the fate which has ordained that we must resist this new and terrible despotism amid the confusions in Asia created by the mistakes of our recent history and by the impingement of a technical upon a nontechnical culture.

Fortunately, the "common people" of the nation have the wisdom and common sense which the hysterical nationalists lack. They measure the hazards and the imponderables of our situation more correctly than some political leaders. Fortunately also the President, despite vacillations on many issues, seems clear on this paramount issue. His long experience with European defense and his intimate contact with the statesmen of Europe give him a wholesome perspective on the issues. Whether he can succeed in getting through the Formosan crisis without a war is of course, a question, for he must satisfy our European allies on the one hand and Senator Knowland on the other. The Chinese Communists, meanwhile, seem intent on proving his policy wrong and Senator Knowland's right.

5. *The United Nations and the Free World*

The moral implications of the relation of our nation to the United Nations are often overlooked or depreciated because that portion of our citizenship which is most anxious to express its loyalty to the principle of international order is also most inclined to be impatient with the limitations of the present United Nations organization as an instrument of world order. Actually the United Nations is a very good instrument for the expression of two basic requirements for any great moral endeavor. William James once defined the two requirements as (a) Resoluteness in the original commitment to the cause or discipline and (b) A whole series of specific acts of loyalty to give historical body to the commitment.

When the United Nations was launched at San Francisco in 1945 our readiness to commit ourselves to it represented a new chapter in the spiritual pilgrimage of our nation. The tragedies of World War II had convinced many peoples, and not merely us, that world community was waiting to become actual, that the days of unqualified national sovereignty were over and that it was important to have such a constitutional instrument of world order. We in America, more than in other nations, felt our commitment to the United Nations to have the spiritual significance of the first part of William James' formula. We had been involved in an almost pathological isolationism in the long armistice between the two wars, believing that we could preserve our innocency by the rigor of our efforts to avoid embroilment in world conflict; and yet we were darkly conscious that an ignoble irresponsibility was compounded with a hardly less noble effort to be "pure."

The same technical civilization which was drawing the world together into a community of common destiny was also making us the most powerful of all the nations. We had entered two world wars peripherally. We emerged from the second, incomparably the strongest nation on earth. We had arrived at our maturity in one leap of strength. We were anxious to prove our sense of responsibility to the nascent community of nations, as the measure of our spiritual maturity.

For these reasons we may have invested our

commitment to the United Nations with greater significance than we had the right to ascribe to it. Some of our idealists pretended that the U.N. was really a complete global constitutional system; and others, knowing that it was not, started educational campaigns to make it a more ideal constitutional order, by removing the veto power of the great nations, for instance. But the United Nations fulfilled more than was expected of it precisely because it was less than an ideal system. It was a system of co-operation among the nations designed not for ideal possibilities but for the actualities of the present situation. Therefore, it could not only help us to take a resolute first step in the direction of world order, but could also be the vehicle for all those acts of fidelity in an ongoing relation, which give body to the initial resolution.

Let us compare the broadest and highest of all human communities, the global community, with the smallest and most primordial, the family, in order to test the meaning of both functions. The family is best established if the partnership between a man and a woman is entered on the presupposition that it is irrevocable. If the partnership is presumed to be tentative, there will not be enough resolution to overcome the hazards to its success which the vicissitudes of life always present. I am enough of a modern to believe that there are exceptions to the ideal of the indissolubility of marriage. But I am not so modern as to find much value in the idea of reducing marriage to as tentative a contract as possible. The strength of the original resolution frequently accounts for the success with which a partnership is maintained through many trials which could hardly have been anticipated in the original covenant, even though it contained the words: "for richer, for poorer, for better, for worse."

But an original covenant soon fades if it is not given substance by those daily acts of fidelity and forbearance through which lives are wedded and amalgamated. We Americans are inclined to a rather abstract type of idealism. Therefore it is more important for us to emphasize the second, rather than the first, part of James' formula. The United Nations has become one (and the chief) of many devices by which we are trying to organize our world. The "our" has of course achieved a special significance since the San Francisco charter. It means the "free" world; the non-Communist world. Since we entered into the original covenant a momentous and tragic event has occurred. The Russian-Communist world has made it clear beyond peradventure of doubt that it still holds to its secular utopian world religion which some had rather foolishly and furtively believed to have been dissipated by our wartime partnership. But almost immediately after San Francisco the Russians began to make it clear that they divided the world into two camps, an "evil capitalist" and a "good Communist" one. Nothing could be quite so implausible as this Communist version of good and evil, of human nature and human destiny. That it should have been introduced into world history at a particular moment when it would further confuse an already difficult task of organizing the world belongs to the most tragic aspects of contemporary history.

This fact is so tragic that many people in the Western world cannot bear to accept it, and they entertain various theories which are intended to veil and obscure the tragic situation. We have heard men propose in the Councils of UNESCO, for instance, that a cultural organization like UNESCO might bridge the chasm which the "politicians" failed to bridge. International conferences to iron out the ideological differences between ourselves and the Russians have been proposed again and again on the assumption that these differences could not be too great because both sides use the same words. But the real

tragedy of the situation lies in the fact that use
of the same words hides a conflict of diametri-
cally opposite ideas. It is difficult, but necessary,
to recognize that the Communist ideology has no
resources within it for coming to terms with
other systems of thought. It is dogmatic without
qualification. It may ultimately yield to the
pressure of world history but it is not likely to be
beguiled by any international conference.

No good purpose is served by minimizing the
tragedy in which we are involved in our struggle
with communism by making ourselves believe
for instance that communism is a slightly more
equalitarian, and ours a slightly more libertarian,
version of a common democratic creed. There
may be some initial similarities between liberal
and Communist utopian illusions; but there are
few similarities between a democratic tentativity
and modesty in holding to our various beliefs
and the Communist fanaticism in which a monopoly of power unites with illusory hopes to
breed cruelty and hatred.

This division of the world was not foreseen
when we accepted the charter at San Francisco.
But fortunately institutions, though they may be
abstractly conceived, have a way of being
formed by the actual events of history, or rather
they have a way of being reformed if only we

remain loyal to the original motive rather than the original pattern. In a world thus tragically divided the United Nations organization has taken on functions which correspond to the new necessities. On the one hand, it is a minimal bridge between the Communist and the free world. On the other hand, it is an organ for integrating the free world. The Security Council is the symbol of the one function, and the General Assembly of the other. There are those who regard this double function as not sufficiently neat. They would like an organization which would organize the non-Communist world more effectively than the United Nations can. They are impatient with an organization which cannot speak unequivocally on many issues.

But let us avoid all neat solutions which try to make the realities more logical than they are. We have a double duty to avoid war and to prevent the spread of Communist tyranny. These two duties are not necessarily incompatible. But it is important that we impress the world with our interest in both. To preserve a minimal bridge between ourselves and Russia requires the preservation of the United Nations organization. We are suspected in some parts of the world of being more anxious to win an eventual war than to avoid its outbreak. This may be a misinterpretation of our true mind; or it may be a natural suspicion of the nation which has primary responsibility for the military defenses of the free world. But however natural the suspicions and the misinterpretations, we cannot afford to be guilty of any act or attitude which gives them credence. An atomic war is so terrible in its known and unknown consequences that no stone must be left unturned for its avoidance. The idea of a preventive war sometimes tempts minds, whose primary preoccupation is the military defense of a nation and who think it might be prudent to pick the most propitious moment for the start of what they regard as inevitable hostilities. But the rest of us must resist such ideas with every moral resource. Nothing in history is inevitable, including the probable. So long as war has not broken out, we still have the possibility of avoiding it. Those who think that there is little difference between a cold and a hot war are either knaves or fools; for there is an obvious difference between a state of tension and a state of destruction and mutual annihilation.

Our loyalty to the United Nations is not the only way of proving our patience and lack of hysteria. But it is one effective method.

The other function of the United Nations is

the integration of the so-called free world. This process of integration requires various institutions. The Atlantic community now has the NATO defense organization. The technical assistance program of the U. N., of UNESCO, and of our own government functions through various instrumentalities. But the General Assembly has become the chief global parliament, where the policies and sentiments of nations are submitted to the scrutiny of world opinion and where every particular national interest must meet the test of its compatibility with the unity and order of the community of free nations. It is in this context that we have our opportunity to fill out our original commitment with acts of fidelity in specific situations.

It is significant that despite the deep chasm in the world community, the United Nations has helped the new state of Israel to come into being and it was active in solving the Arab refugee problem which followed in the wake of that settlement. It is, of course, not possible for the United Nations to solve the problem of the chasm between Russia and the non-Communist world. When basic mutual trust is lacking no constitutional device can create community. We have had two experiences, one during the Berlin air-lift and then in Korea, in which we have learned how difficult it is to reach even minimal agreements when we do not trust each other. But there is a considerable degree of mutual trust in the free world. In that world constitutional instruments can implement mutual trust; and trust can furnish the foundation for the laws, constitutions, and arrangements.

I am sure that it will not be surprising or shocking to Americans to know that one of the primary tasks of the United Nations and its various agencies is to relate American power to a weakened world and American prosperity to an impoverished world. The degree of power held in and by America in the free world is in fact an historical development, almost as unexpected as the division of the world by communism. We and the world knew that American power was great; but we are only beginning to appreciate how preponderant our power is. This preponderance is an immediate resource for the strength of the free world. But it is also a hazard. Power and weakness do not march easily in the same harness. It tempts the holders of power to pride and it tempts the weak to envy and resentment.

We Americans must accustom ourselves to being unpopular in the world. There will be some good reasons for our unpopularity and some bad

ones. The good reasons will be that we shall
make mistakes in the use of our power, because
it impinges everywhere in the world, far beyond
our conscious contriving. That is why it is important to have as many checks upon its exercise
as possible. The bad reasons for our unpopularity
will be that Communist propaganda will seek to
interpret the difference between our prosperity
and the world's poverty as due to exploitation.
This explanation contains hardly a modicum of
truth; for the differences in living standards are
due primarily to differences of production standards in technical and agrarian societies. The
propaganda against us achieves a special plausibility in Asia where resentments against past
imperialism and colonialism are compounded
with envy of our wealth and power. Not many
exploitative elements are left in the old imperialism; and in any case we were not directly involved in it. But we are the symbol of the whole
Western world in the eyes of Asia and we inherit
past resentments even as we must bear the brunt
of present envies.

While the Communists give an interpretation
of this difference between our wealth and the
world's poverty which is as false as it is plausible,
we must be intent to give a right answer to the
problems raised by the contrast. We must help

the impoverished world to gain greater technical efficiency, and must strengthen every political instrument of common living which allays suspicions and resentments. We cannot overcome all the hazards to mutual understanding between ourselves and an impoverished world in both Europe and Asia; but we can learn in actual encounters to deal loyally with our allies in the free world. From such loyalty will spring policies, which we must refrain from calling generous because they will be in our own long-term interest; but they will be wise in the sense that they will help to cement the unity of the free world.

Our actions and attitudes on detailed questions of daily policy, on questions of tariffs and immigration quotas, on technical assistance programs and investment in undeveloped areas will contribute more to the international community, which all far-seeing Americans see in the making, than any abstract commitments to ideal and impossible world constitutions which some idealistic Americans regard as important. World community must gradually grow through acts of mutual loyalty. Mutual loyalty in situations of great disproportions of power and fortune is difficult but not impossible. It is one of the marks of our political immaturity that many Americans should regard it a simple matter for us to be related to continents in the turmoil of revolutions, of economic and social revolutions piled upon ethnic and political ones. If anything goes wrong in Asia or Africa, that is, if anything develops which is not according to our tastes or according to our interests, someone always rises to ask, "What error did the State Department commit this time?"

We are in the throes of vast forces beyond the control of any single agency or power. We can deflect, harness, and beguile the historical forces of our age but we cannot ignore, defy, or annul them. Perhaps no lesson is more important for a nation as powerful as we, than the truth that even powerful nations cannot master their own destiny; for they are in a web of history in which many desires, hopes, wills, and ambitions, other than their own, are operative.

Perhaps this is the most important lesson for us to learn in our relation to the world community, because we are, as a nation, not accustomed to the frustrations of history. We have grown from infancy to adolescence and from adolescence to maturity in quick and easy strides; and we were inclined to solve every problem, as young people do, by increasing our strength. Now we have suddenly come upon a

mystery of life. It is that an infant in his cradle
is in some respects more powerful than a man in
his maturity. For the infant's every wish is
fulfilled by some benevolent attendant; but
the wishes of a mature man are subject to
the hazards of many conflicting and competing
desires. We were stronger as a nation when we
rocked in the cradle of our continental security
than we are today when we "bestride this nar-
row world like a huge colossus," for the patterns
of history have grown more rapidly than our
strength. This is no counsel to engage in the
abortive effort to recapture our childhood. Thank
God, that whatever new temptations may assail
us, we have overcome that particular temptation.

But we do face another, even more dangerous,
temptation. That is to become impatient with the
slow, tortuous and sometimes contradictory processes of history and thus to bring our history to
a tragic conclusion by seeking to bring our contemporary pattern of history to a logical one. We
must learn to bear the burdens of our day, including the burdens of a heavy taxation and the
anxieties of a cold war, without any certain
knowledge how our acts of fidelity to a nascent
community of nations may be rewarded or justified. Martin Buber, the great Jewish philosopher,
observed recently that the one difference be-

tween our encounter with the Nazis and our encounter with communism was that we were quite
certain, even when the Nazis were at their
height, that their doom was sure. We also know
that a world order based upon Communist force
and fraud cannot finally prevail; but we are not
so certain when and how it will disintegrate.
When a political movement mixes utopian illusions with force and fraud one cannot be certain
how much time will be required for its victims
to revolt or its accomplices to become disillu-
sioned. We must move upon an uphill road without knowing the length of the road or without
being assured of the easement of our burden at
the summit.

Let us, therefore, in conducting our educational program, be less concerned with the principles of international loyalty in the abstract and
more intent to deal realistically with every concrete issue which faces our nation. In some of
these issues a powerful nation will be inclined to
disregard the wishes of weaker allies. In some of
them a proud nation will be inclined to resent
criticism of envious or resentful friends. In some
of them a frustrated nation will be inclined to
become impatient with the slow processes of
history. In some of them a nation fearful of the
future will be inclined to "fly the evils that it

knows not of" in its desire to avoid the "slings and arrows of outrageous fortune."

Our nation is basically committed to the principles of a co-operative world community. The real problem is whether we can give this basic commitment the body of, the flesh and blood of, our daily acts of loyalty and forbearance in the nascent community of mankind. Undoubtedly the constitutional instruments of world order must be perfected in time. But the more perfect instruments must grow out of the more perfect mutualities of daily living together.

If our nation is to achieve success in this arduous and sometimes disheartening task we must not give way to the "cry-baby" theory of modern history which regrets the trials and tumults of our era and wishes that the lot of our generation had been cast in a more pleasant century. The trials are undoubtedly great, and the insecurities and frustrations are disheartening; but the stakes are also very big and the possibilities of achievement are inspiring. They might well prompt our generation to Rupert Brook's prayer of thanksgiving: "God be thanked who matched us with this hour."

6. *The Illusion of World Government* *

I

The trustful acceptance of false solutions for our perplexing problems adds a touch of pathos to the tragedy of our age.

The tragic character of our age is revealed in the world-wide insecurity which is the fate of modern man. Technical achievements, which a previous generation had believed capable of solving every ill to which the human flesh is heir, have created, or at least accentuated, our insecurity. For the growth of technics has given the perennial problem of our common life a more complex form and a scope that has grown to be world-wide.

Our problem is that technics have established a rudimentary world community but have not integrated it organically, morally, or politically.

* Reprinted by permission from FOREIGN AFFAIRS, April, 1949. Copyright by Council on Foreign Relations, Inc., New York.

They have created a community of mutual dependence, but not one of mutual trust and respect. Without this higher integration, advancing technics tend to sharpen economic rivalries within a general framework of economic interdependence; they change the ocean barriers of yesterday into the battlegrounds of today; and they increase the deadly efficacy of the instruments of war so that vicious circles of mutual fear may end in atomic conflicts and mutual destruction. To these perplexities an ideological conflict has been added, which divides the world into hostile camps.

It is both necessary and laudable that men of good will should, in this situation, seek to strengthen every moral and political force which might give a rudimentary world community a higher degree of integration. It was probably inevitable that the desperate plight of our age should persuade some well-meaning men that the gap between a technically integrated and politically divided community could be closed by the simple expedient of establishing a world government through the fiat of the human will and creating world community by the fiat of world government. It is this hope which adds a touch of pathos to already tragic experiences.

The hope not only beguiles some men from urgent moral and political responsibilities. It tempts others into irresponsible criticisms of the necessary minimal constitutional structure which we have embodied in the United Nations and which is as bad as its critics aver only if a better one is within the realm of possibilities.

Virtually all arguments for world government rest upon the simple presupposition that the desirability of world order proves the attainability of world government. Our precarious situation is unfortunately no proof, either of the moral ability of mankind to create a world government by an act of the will, nor of the political ability of such a government to integrate a world community in advance of a more gradual growth of the "social tissue" which every community requires more than government.

Most advocates of world government also assume that nations need merely follow the alleged example of the individuals of another age who are supposed to have achieved community by codifying their agreements into law and by providing an agency of some kind for law enforcement. This assumption ignores the historic fact that the mutual respect for each other's rights in particular communities is older than any code

of law; and that machinery for the enforcement
of law can be efficacious only when a community
as a whole obeys its laws implicitly, so that
coercive enforcement may be limited to a recalcitrant minority.

The fallacy of world government can be stated
in two simple propositions. The first is that
governments are not created by fiat (though
sometimes they can be imposed by tyranny).
The second is that governments have only
limited efficacy in integrating a community.

II

The advocates of world government talk of
calling a world constitutional convention which
would set up the machinery of a global constitutional order and would then call upon the
nations to abrogate or abridge their sovereignty
in order that this newly created universal sovereignty could have unchallenged sway. No such
explicit abnegation has ever taken place in the
history of the world. Explicit governmental authority has developed historically from the implicit authority of patriarchal or matriarchal
tribal forms. Governments, so established, have
extended their dominion over weaker neighbors.
But the abridgment of sovereignty has always

been indirect rather than direct; or it has been attained by the superimposition of power.

The notion that world government is a fairly simple possibility is the final and most absurd form of the "social contract" conception of government which has confused modern political thought since Hobbes. It must certainly be obvious by this time that the conception of a state of nature in which all men were at war with all, and of a subsequent social contract through which men established a power over themselves to avoid mutual annihilation, is a pure fiction. A small human community is as primordial as the individual. No group of individuals has ever created either government or community out of whole cloth. One reason that the social contract conception of government has a particular plausibility with us is that the United States came closer to a birth by "contract" than any other nation. But the preamble of our constitution declares that its purpose is to establish a "more perfect union." That is a very telling phrase which presupposes a previous union. This previous union was in fact established on the battlefield in a common struggle against a common foe; it needed only to be made "more perfect." It may be observed in passing

that, though the thirteen colonies had never en-
joyed sovereignty, they did not find it too easy
to submit what had only been potential, and not
actual, sovereignty to the authority of the federal
union. We fought a civil war before it was
proved that they had in fact done this without
reservations.

When the question is raised whether the nations of the world would voluntarily first create,
and then submit to, a supernational authority,
the possible reluctance of nations, other than
Russia, to take this step is fortunately or unfortunately obscured by the Russian intransigeance. The Russians have declared again and
again that they would leave the United Nations
if the veto power were abolished. This means
that Russia, as a prospective minority in a world
community, is not ready to submit her fate to
the will of a majority, even in such a loose
organization as the United Nations. It is therefore obvious that she would be even more un-
willing to submit her sovereignty to a more
highly integrated constitutional order.

The proponents of world government have
two answers to the problem posed by Russian
intransigence. One is to assert that the Russians
never have had the chance to accept or reject a

genuinely constitutional world order; and that there are real possibilities of her acceptance of a constitution which is not weighted against her. This answer contains in a nutshell the rationalist illusion implicit in world government theories. It assumes that constitutions can insure the mutual trust upon which community rests. Actually, even the best constitution must, if it is democratic, set up some kind of majority rule. It is not workable if there is not enough common ground between majority and minority to assure that a majority will not take advantage of a minority, or that the minority will not suspect the majority of injustice, even though without cause. There are republics in South America with quite nice constitutions in which a defeated minority starts conspiracies against the government, usually through military channels, on the day after election.

The other answer to the problem of Russian intransigeance is a proposed creation of a "world" government without Russia. Thus in the name of "one world" the world would be divided in two. Proponents of world government are always ready with criticisms of the ambiguities in the Charter of the United Nations, without recognizing that those ambiguities correspond to the actual historical situation. The Security Council is, for instance, a bridge of a sort between the segments of a divided world. They would destroy that bridge for the sake of creating a more logical constitutional system. This done, they look forward to one of two possibilities.

One is that Russia, faced with a united opposition, and concluding that she would not have to sacrifice her Communist Government but only her ambition to spread communism, would ultimately capitulate and join the world federation. This abstract approach to political problems is completely oblivious of the dynamism of communism.

The other course chosen by some advocates of world government is to create such a government without Russia and to divide the world more consistently in the name of the principle of "one" world. If this should lead to a world conflict they believe that the agonies of war will be assuaged for us by our knowledge that we are at least fighting for a principle of ultimate validity.

There is, of course, a possibility that a closer political integration of the non-Communist nations may save the world from war by the creation of an adequate preponderance of power in the west. But such an objective is not to be reached by loftily disavowing "power politics" in favor of "law." The world federalists who accept the inevitability of war walk bravely up the hill of pure idealism and down again into the realm of pure power politics. In this journey they rid themselves of the logical and moral ambiguities of the much despised quasiconstitutional system of the United Nations. Their brethren who are in a less exalted frame of mind will continue to put up with the Charter for the sake of preserving a bridge, however slight, between Russia and the west, making the best arrangements they can to restrain Russia, while trying at the same time to strengthen the existing world security agencies.

The ambiguities in the Charter of the United Nations which so outrage the advocates of world government are in fact the consequence of seeking to guarantee two, rather than one, objectives. The one objective is to preserve the unity of one world, even though it be seriously divided, and to provide a meeting ground between east and west where some of the tensions and frictions may be resolved. The other is to preserve the integrity of our "way of life" against a tyrannical system which we abhor. The Russians, in so far as they are honest devotees of a Marxist dream of world order, are presumably in the same position. Each of us hopes ultimately to create a world order upon the basis of our conception of justice. Neither of us is ready, at the moment, to submit our fate to a world authority without reservation, so long as the possibility remains that such an authority could annul a system of law and justice to which we are deeply committed.

III

So far we have considered only the difficulties of creating a world government by constitutional fiat. But a much more serious defect in world government theories is to be found in their conception of the relation of government to community. Governments cannot create communities for the simple reason that the authority of government is not primarily the authority of law nor the authority of force, but the authority of the community itself. Laws are obeyed because the community accepts them as corresponding, on the whole, to its conception of justice. This is particularly true of democratically organized communities. But it is well to observe that even

in traditional nondemocratic communities of the
past there was a discernible difference between
tyranny and legitimate government. It consisted
precisely in the fact that a legitimate government
relied primarily upon the implicit consent of the
community.

Even in a national constitutional system, such
as our own, we have seen how limited is the
power of law whenever a portion of the community adheres to moral standards which differ
from those of the total community. We have had
this experience both with the prohibition movement and with the question of civil rights for
Negroes in southern states. And where is the
police force, loyal to a world state, to come from?
The police power of a government cannot be a
pure political artifact. It is an arm of the community's body. If the body is in pieces the arm
cannot integrate it.

The priority of the community to its laws and
its use of force does not mean that both law and
force may not have limited efficacy in perfecting
the organization and preserving the integrity of
the community. Good constitutions provide for
the rational arbitrament of many conflicting and
competing forces which might otherwise tear the
community apart. Preponderant force in one part

of the community may also so shape the social forces of the total community that its use need not be perpetual. Thus the preponderant force of the northern states decided the issue whether our nation was a nation or merely a federation of states. But force is no longer necessary to guarantee the loyalty of the southern states to our union. The ancient empires of Egypt, Babylon and Persia were created through the preponderant force of a particular city-state; but they finally achieved a unity which did not require the constant application of force. It must be noted that this pattern of coalescence of communities gives us no analogy for the creation of a world community in democratic terms, that is, without the imposition of preponderant power. The best analogy for our present world situation is to be found in Greece rather than in Egypt or Babylon. The Greek city-states never achieved the imperial unity of the oriental empires. The threat of Persia did finally prompt the organization of the Delian League; but the rivalry of Sparta and Athens for the hegemony in the League resulted in its disintegration. The unity of Greece was finally achieved under Philip and Alexander of Macedon. But this imperial unity was also a tyrannical nemesis for Greek culture. The analogy in present global terms would be the final unification of the world through the preponderant power of either America or Russia, whichever proved herself victorious in a final global struggle. The analogy teaches us nothing about the possibilities of a constitutional world state. It may teach us that though the perils of international anarchy are very great, they may still be preferable to international tyranny.

The coalescence of communities from city-states to empires in the ancient world, and from feudal entities to nations in the modern period, was frequently accomplished only by the imposition of preponderant power. The fact is particularly significant, since all these communities could rely upon all sorts of "organic" factors for their force of cohesion which the rudimentary world community lacks. By organic factors, I mean such forces as the power of ethnic kinship, the forces of a common history—particularly the memory of joint struggles against a common foe—a common language, a common culture, and a common religion. We do have examples of ethnically and religiously pluralistic nations and empires, but they possess a basic homogeneity of some kind, underlying the differences. In modern India, where religious differences are thoroughgoing and highly localized, it proved impossible to construct a constitutional system which could allay the mutual fears of Hindus and Moslems. The birth in blood of these two nations, once the unifying force of an imperial power was removed, ought to teach our world planners more about the limited efficacy of constitutions than they have evidently learned. There were certainly more common elements in the situation in India than the world community will possess for a long time to come. Despite these common elements, the unity of India proved to be unattainable.

Sometimes the world planners recognize the absence of organic forces of cohesion in the world community. Thus Erich Kahler† sees that a world constitution lacks the "substratum" of organic and historical forces which characterize the constitutions of national governments. But he draws the conclusion that a world constitution "must create the substratum to which it is to be applied." The proposed method of creating the substratum, according to Mr. Kahler, is to use

† Erich Kahler, "The Question of a 'Minimum Constitution.'" *Common Cause*, June, 1948.

"regions" rather than "extant states" as electoral
units in the world constitution, for "if we base
the world government on the states, we will fail
in the essential task of creating the substratum."
The illusions of omnipotence which infect the
thought of this kind of political idealism could
not be more vividly portrayed. There is no
explanation of how states, who have a sovereign voice, would be persuaded to grant this
electoral power to "regions" which would have
no such voice in a world constitutional convention. The idea probably is that there would be a
nonrepresentative constitutional convention of
"experts" and the hope is that sovereign states
will meekly accept the dictum of the experts that
regions offer a better "substratum" for the world
community than extant states. Nor is any attempt
made to deal with the difficulty that many of the
regions which would hopefully be created are so
little integrated that an electoral canvass would
be completely meaningless in them.

The fact is that even the wisest statecraft cannot create social tissue. It can cut, sew and re-
design social fabric to a limited degree. But the
social fabric upon which it works must be
"given."

IV

The international community is not totally lacking in social tissue; but it is very scant, compared with that of particular states. Let us briefly assess the various factors in it. Very important as a force of social cohesion in the world community is the increasing economic interdependence of peoples of the world. But it is important to contrast this economic interdependence immediately with the wide disparity in the economic strength of various nations. At the climactic dinner of the World Republic convention, held in Chicago in October, 1948, Professor Urey, the atomic scientist, expressed the conviction that the "inclusion of the illiterate, poverty-stricken, overnumerous masses of the Far East" constituted the major problem of the world state. He believed that the white race would not tolerate being outvoted by Asiatics. He therefore proposed a system of weighted votes in favor of nations with high literacy and abundance of raw materials and industrial production. He felt certain that the more "enlightened" Orientals would not object to this procedure. But an objection, from Thomas Tchou, sitting two places to the left of Professor Urey, was immediately forthcoming. Weighted representation, he declared, was immoral.‡ Thus the real problems have an inconvenient habit of peeking through, even at a dinner of a World Republic convention.

A second factor in the social tissue of the world community is the fear of mutual annihilation, heightened in recent years by the new dimension which atomic discoveries have given to mankind's instruments of death. We must not underestimate this fear as a social force, even as we must recognize that some culturally pluralistic communities of past history have achieved some cohesion through the minimal conviction that order is to be preferred to anarchy. But the fear of destruction in itself is less potent than the fear of specific peril from a particular foe. There is no record in history of peoples establishing a common community because they feared each other, though there are many instances when the fear of a common foe acted as the cement of cohesion.

The final and most important in the social tissue of the world community is a moral one. Enlightened men in all nations have some sense of obligation to their fellow men, beyond the limits of their nation-state. There is at least an

‡ *Common Cause*, December, 1948, p. 199.

inchoate sense of obligation to the inchoate community of mankind. The desperate necessity for a more integrated world community has undoubtedly increased this sense of obligation, inculcated in the conscience of mankind since the rise of universal, rather than parochial, philosophies and religions. This common moral sense is of tremendous importance for the moral and religious life of mankind; but it does not have so much immediate political relevance as is sometimes supposed. Political cohesion requires common convictions on particular issues of justice; and these are lacking. If there is a "natural law" which is "self-evident" to all men, it certainly does not contain very much specific content beyond such minimal rules as the prohibition of murder and theft and such general principles of justice as the dictum that each man is to have his due. There is little agreement on the criteria by which the due of each man is to be measured.

There is a special irony in the fact that the primary differences in the conceptions of justice in the world do not, however, spring from religious and cultural differences between East and West. They can, therefore, not be resolved by elaborate efforts at cultural syncretism between

East and West. The primary differences arise from a civil war in the heart of Western civilization, in which a fanatical equalitarian creed has been pitted against a libertarian one. This civil war has become nationally localized. Russia has become the national center of the equalitarian creed, and America is the outstanding proponent of the libertarian one. The common use of the word "democracy," together with the contradictory interpretations of the meaning of that word, is the semantic symbol of the conflict. The idea that this conflict could be resolved by greater semantic accuracy is, however, one of the illusions of a too nationalistic culture which fails to understand the power of the social forces expressed in contradictory symbols.

In short, the forces which are operating to integrate the world community are limited. To call attention to this fact does not mean that all striving for a higher and wider integration of the world community is vain. That task must and will engage the conscience of mankind for ages to come. But the edifice of government which we build will be sound and useful if its height is proportionate to the strength of the materials from which it is constructed. The immediate political situation requires that we seek not only peace, but also the preservation of a civilization which we hold to be preferable to the universal tyranny with which Soviet aggression threatens us. Success in this double task is the goal; let us not be diverted from it by the pretense that there is a simple alternative.

There is obviously no political program which can offer us, in our situation, perfect security against either war or tyranny. Nevertheless we are not prisoners of historical destiny. We shall have constant opportunity to perfect instruments of peace and justice if we succeed in creating some communal foundation upon which constitutional structures can rest. We shall exploit our opportunities the more successfully, however, if we have knowledge of the limits of the will in creating government, and of the limits of government in creating community. We may have pity upon, but can have no sympathy with, those who flee to the illusory security of the impossible from the insecurities and ambiguities of the possible.

7. *The Limits of Cultural Co-operation*

I have just returned from serving as a member of the American delegation at the fourth annual conference of UNESCO—an outsider privileged for several weeks to be on the inside. The two out-standing impressions in my mind after survey-ing the far-flung activities of UNESCO, as out-lined at this conference, have to do with the technical efficiency of its work on the one hand, and with its ideological weakness on the other hand. The tasks which UNESCO undertakes in the technical field comprise two primary forms of activity: that of giving help in educational methods and materials and in methods of com-munication to undeveloped countries, and that of removing various types of barriers to the free flow of communication between all peoples. This work is wholly admirable. Educational missions to backward regions have provided new stand-ards and methods for school systems; and the technical assistance program seeks to bring technically advanced nations to the assistance of less advanced nations in every field of education and communication. The work dealing with the removal of barriers includes such tasks as working toward more uniform and less restrictive copyright laws in all nations; providing for a greater number of translations of classics in all languages; removing tariffs on all materials used in education; encouraging the exchange of art exhibits and of great orchestras; delving into comparative folklore; encouraging the formation of international organizations in almost every discipline of human culture; and providing for an ever-wider system of student and academic exchanges. This catalogue is only a small sample of the projects which are under way in UNESCO in the two fields of assistance to weaker nations and of freeing the lines of communication between all nations.

The problem of our day is how to integrate the world community. Communication does not of itself create community; but there can be no community without communication. One might even maintain that communication does of itself create minimal community, though it must always be recognized that communication may be the bearer of hostility as well as of amity. In so far as this is the problem, UNESCO is a mighty instrument, mutually used by the nations to make technics the servant of communication as they are already the servants of commerce. It does not guarantee peace, as some enthusiasts for UNESCO assert. Even the more integral community of nations may be rent asunder by specific conflicts. If nations refuse, for instance, to engage in a process of communication as Russia does, there is nothing in the process itself which overcomes the recalcitrance of such a nation.

These impressive achievements are enough to justify the organization. However, I would not be truthful if I did not record my convictions of a certain ideological weakness in the organization. But I must add immediately that an organization which must deal with the cultural pluralism of a world community is almost bound to be ideologically weak. The ideological weakness is at least partly explained by the difficulty of finding a spiritual basis for the unity of mankind in a pluralistic world. The former Director General Julian Huxley tried to commit the organization to a kind of synthetic world culture based upon scientific humanism. This explicit attempt was resisted. But implicitly that is where UNESCO still stands ideologically, if it stands anywhere. In a series of three public debates, designed to elucidate these more ultimate problems, in which I had the honor to participate for our delegation, four speakers expressed the conviction that the universality of the natural sciences was the bedrock upon which universal humanism would gradually develop. This is an old illusion, expressed possibly in its most classical form by Comte. It is an illusion because universality of the rational principles underlying science is no antidote to the relativity of cultural viewpoints when one moves from the form to the content of rational propositions. It was interesting to find that confidence in science as a basis of brotherhood, which is sometimes regarded by Europeans as the mark of the immaturity of American culture, should have such a world-wide acceptance.

Another illusion frequently expressed among delegates is the belief that higher standards of literacy and education or more adequate means of communication are the guarantors of peace. In the opening session, the chairman of the executive board, the Indian Ambassador to Moscow, thought that the unresolved conflict between Russia and the West might be resolved if it were taken out of the hands of politicians and men of culture were asked to resolve it. This proposal assumed that men of culture could be .ound in Russia who would not represent the political viewpoint of the Russian oligarchy. But the suggestion involves an even more serious mistake which is very dear to the heart of many moderns. It is the belief that the difficulties which statesmen face in guiding their nations are due, not so much to their responsible relation to their several nations, as to their intellectual inferiority in comparison with cultural leaders. This misses the whole point in the encounter of nations with each other. Such an encounter is a power-political one, in which statesmen distinguish themselves from philosophers and scientists, not by their smaller degree of intelligence but by their higher degree of responsibility to their respective communities.

The difficulty with UNESCO on the ideological side is in short that its idealism is informed by a too simple universalism. Its idealists suppress the tragic realities of life, the conflicts of interests which cannot be easily composed, the perils of war which cannot be simply overcome, the power of collective egotism which is not easily sublimated. These weaknesses are a proof of the thesis that the point of conflict between the Christian faith and modern idealism is exactly at the same place where St. Paul found the conflict between the Jewish legalism of his day and his faith: "Thou knowest the law," he said to the legalists of his day, "thou makest a boast of it to God. Thou knowest thou shalt not kill, dost thou not kill?"

It is interesting to note that the men who deal with the actual realities of politics tend to criticize the purposes of UNESCO at precisely the same point where a Christian would have to criticize it. They think of it as a collection of unrealistic star gazers who are not willing to face the brutal facts of life. This ideological weakness might be corrected. It will, in fact, be corrected by the very realities of contemporary experience which have already dissipated so much of the simple faith of the eighteenth century in the goodness of rational man. But in that case, what will become of the idealism? Will it survive? The spiritual problem of UNESCO is in short the spiritual problem of modern man, who must find a way of engaging in impossible tasks and not be discouraged when he fails to complete any of them.

Spiritually an organization such as UNESCO,

as well as the whole modern generation, really
needs a faith which recognizes the completion of
life within and above its fragmentariness, the
final solution beyond all our solutions. It needs,
in short, an apprehension of the grace which
makes it possible for men to say, "We are per-
plexed but not unto despair."

However, we must not assume that it would
be possible simply to offer UNESCO what we
regard as the resources of the Christian faith as
the basis of world community. Let us admit that
shallow notes in the thought of modern inter-
nationalism are almost inevitable consequences of
the cultural and religious pluralism of the world
community. It must strive desperately after minimal common conceptions of justice or it will be
unable to order its common life. But it can certainly not achieve common convictions on the
very meaning of life. It will embody in its complex unity, for a long time to come, Confucian
humanism, Indian pantheism, Mohammedan
legalism, and both Marxist and liberal forms of
modern secularism. This is an embarrassing
situation because the problems which a great
international organization faces constantly confront men with the ultimate issues of life. Here
is an organization which seeks to realize the

impossible: a world community. It must not regard this end as a simple possibility; but neither can it dismiss the task as an impossibility. It stands, therefore, constantly at the final limit of the human situation where the possible and the impossible are curiously intermingled and where it is difficult to distinguish between God's and our possibilities.

In such a situation a Christian who deeply feels the inadequacies of a too simple humanism must nevertheless loyally participate in the practical tasks which must be done. It would be better if they were done without illusion. Yet if some should be driven by utopian illusions to do them they may well be counted more worthy in God's sight than those who have given up both responsibilities and illusions.

It is to be hoped that UNESCO's many seminars on cultural problems will ultimately draw into their studies of basic issues, not merely the only slightly varying thought of philosophers and scientists who, however varied their national background, stand on the common ground of modern secularism, but will be willing to let Christians (both Catholic and Protestant) contribute their own particular insights. The other world religions must of course also be heard. But if modern secularism is not to regard the Christian faith as a simple irrelevance in the great issues which face modern man, Christians must probably take the initiative. We have a duty toward this organization not only to support it in technical fields in which it is strong, but to seek to correct it in the field of theory where it betrays the weaknesses, both of our contemporary culture and of a religiously plural world community, which is tempted to reduce its variety to a shallow lowest common denominator. If "peoples speak to peoples" this communication must finally include debate on the ultimate issues of life and not meaningless agreement on shallow generalities about the unity of mankind.

8. *The Limits of Military Power*

As we receive day-by-day news of the agonies of disunity and potential chaos which Southeast Asia is undergoing in its struggle for order and unity, it is well to remember that, only a few short years ago, our whole nation was excited by the crisis in the war between Vietnam and the Communists involving the obscure fort of Dienbienphu. The fortress was besieged, and we were given to understand that its fall would seriously alter the whole strategic picture in Asia. Vice President Nixon, speaking to an editors' dinner, hinted that it would probably be necessary to support the French military effort if catastrophe was to be avoided. The Administration seemed on the verge of committing at least our Air Force to this struggle. President Eisenhower, standing on the brink of war, finally retreated—partly because he had the sixth sense to know that such a commitment would not be popular, and partly because the Senatorial leaders were reluctant to give him the authority. In any event, we seemed about committed to "save" the last bastion of freedom by military action.

No doubt military action must frequently be the *ultima ratio* in a struggle with a foe. We saved the whole situation by prompt military action in Korea. But the contemporary situation in Vietnam should certainly instruct us on the limits of military power in the long cold war. For what we are witnessing is the revelation of the poverty of our cause in moral and political terms in a nation which we sought to save from Communist aggression by military defense. That poverty is revealed by the still-lingering resentment against French imperialism, by the opposition to the puppet "Chief of State" Bao Dai on the part of the people of the budding nation, and by their own inability to achieve unity against divisive forces within their nation. The Government's desperate victory over military formations which are alternately described as "river pirates" and "religious sects" reveals the lack of solidity and unity in the community; and the trouble with Bao Dai, regarded as a puppet of the French, is a reminder of the old trouble which made the Vietnamese struggle against communism so ineffective. Military power is, in short, ineffective when it lacks a moral and political base. It is the fist of a hand; but the hand must be attached to an arm, and the arm to a body; and the body must be robust before the fist can be effective.

Military power is, therefore, necessary, particularly in moments of crisis when the community faces recalcitrance and anarchy at home, and dispute with another community abroad. It is more effective in international disputes than in domestic ones because the order and peace of a community is primarily dependent upon forces of cohesion and accommodation for which pure force is an irrelevance. But, even in international disputes, military force has its limits. It is primarily limited by the morale of the community which exercises the force. That is why pure military power was so ineffective in Vietnam and why, incidentally, no amount of military aid could save the Chinese Nationalist cause. It lacked the cohesion and morale to avail itself of the proffered aid.

Despite these obvious limits of military power, the American nation has become strangely enamored with military might. We treat the Asian continent with its nationalistic and social upheavals, as if it were possible to establish order out of chaos by the assertion of military might. We are preoccupied with our "defense perimeter" in Asia and have little interest in the vast political complexities of the great continent except to express consistent contempt for the great uncommitted nation, India, though that nation's neutralism is not informed by the slightest degree of sympathy for communism. It is not so certain that it may not possess illusions about this tyranny; but we ought at any rate have more patience with neutralism, particularly since we emerged only so recently from a like mood vis-à-vis Europe.

Our attitude toward India is typical of our indifference toward the political complexities of a continent in ferment, our blindness to the hazards which our cause inevitably faces on that continent. The resentments of the Asian people against the white man's arrogance and against the imperialist impact of a technical civilization are bound to prove handicaps to our cause even when it is contending against a vicious tyranny. These moral and political hazards cannot be overcome by the show of military power. In fact, military might may tend to aggravate our moral and political embarrassments.

Thus, our preoccupation with military power and strategy places us in a false light in Asia, particularly since it creates a picture which seems to conform to the Communist slogans that identify "militarism" and "imperialism" with "capitalism." The question is why we permitted ourselves to appear in this unfavorable light in the whole of Asia. Our nation is singularly innocent of the military tradition and bereft of the military caste traditionally associated with Prussia. Yet we are made to appear in Asian eyes as the new Prussians. There are probably two reasons for this strange turn of events.

The first is the fact that a serious predicament may persuade even a pacific man to rely upon his fists. We are in a serious predicament in Asia and are therefore tempted to rely too much on our fists to extricate ourselves from our seeming hazards.

The second reason is that our leadership in the world is drawn primarily from our economic and the consequent military strength. Economic power can be quickly transmuted into military power, particularly in a technical age, and more particularly in an atomic age. We are therefore tempted to an undue reliance on the obvious might which we possess, particularly since our apprenticeship in the leadership of world affairs has been brief, and we have not had time to accustom ourselves to the acquisition, and to know the importance, of prestige as a source of power; or to learn patience with the endless complexities of loyalties and resentments of traditions and established forms of cohesion which govern the actions of nations.

This impatience is the more grievous because the very technical achievements which have endowed us with superior military power have also given us living standards which are beyond the dreams of avarice of the nontechnical cultures and which militate against our moral prestige. The combination of fear and envy, which our power and good fortune excites, militates against our moral and political prestige, which is the real source of authority in the political realm. This fact is probably the cause of the paradoxical fact that Britain, which only recently divested itself of its Asian empire, is more popular in Asia than we; and that we, who have always been "anti-imperialist" at least in theory if not in consistent practice, are now regarded as the primary exponents of "imperialism" to the nascent nations of Asia.

Having resisted the temptation to resolve the

Indo-Chinese situation purely by force and by the support of a French imperialism which came to terms with the rising tide of nationalism too tardily, we are doing rather better than the French in coping with the complex problems of a nation which desires freedom but cannot find the unity which would give substance to its independence. There are, in fact, suspicions that the French have aggravated the problem of Vietnam both by their support of Bao Dai and by possibly covert support of the rebellious forces. We are certainly more disinterested than the French in desiring only the health of the new nation, and its sufficient strength to ward off the Communist peril from the north. Perhaps we have done well enough to give us a better reputation in Asia as a political, rather than a military, power.

It must be taken for granted that no amount of political skill or wisdom in the tumultuous affairs of the Asian revolution can obviate the necessity of strong military power, nor obscure the importance of our supremacy in atomic weapons. We can not dispense with military power as the *ultima ratio* of international relations. But we do have to keep it in that position of the ultimate instance and not use a meat-axe in situations in which a deft manipulation of loyalties or channeling of aspirations is called for.

It is well to remember that in collective, as well as individual, life the force which coerces the body but does not persuade the will can have only negative significance. It can prevent something which we abhor more than conflict, and it can enforce our will and purpose momentarily on a recalcitrant foe. But the loyalties and cohesions of the community are managed and transfigured not by force but by a wise statecraft. Therefore, our military power can not be as potent as we think in making our world hegemony sufferable either to our friends and allies or to ourselves. Britain learned the limits of force in Ireland and then in India. We have not had comparable lessons, which may be the reason we do not have a comparable wisdom.

9. *What We Can Learn from Sputnik*

The Army has been successful in sending up an earth satellite, and its success has partially quieted the hysteria of hurt pride which afflicted the nation since the rise of the two sputniks. But some jolts, not to our pride but to our complacency, must still exercise their salutary influence. One hopes that the successful Explorer, winging its way in the earth's orbit, will not persuade the nation to forget its early anxieties. Perhaps sober second thoughts will persuade us to transmute anxieties into insights.

The Russian achievements have illumined assumptions that we might not have made had we not been too fat and complacent. To illustrate:

1. Russia is not a "backward" country, except in living standards and political organization. Even the political tyranny is not backward; it is a novel form of harnessing utopian dreams to despotism. We forgot that it required Japan less than a half century to transmute its economy from an agrarian to an industrial and technical

pattern. We were wrong to assume that a technical culture, requiring so many centuries to germinate in the West, could not be transplanted in much shorter time. Russia has been even a little quicker than Japan and probably for a reason which illustrates our second mistake.

2. We were wrong in assuming that despotism excluded democracy in education, at least the democracy of freedom of opportunity. We should have known for a long time that the Russian young people had a passion for education and that the Communist scholarship program, which recruits the bright sons and daughters of peasants for the most advanced scientific training, is better—that is, more "Jeffersonian"— than our system of free education. We give everyone the right to acquire an education if the family budget and the resourcefulness of the youth are able to cope with our ever-higher educational costs. That is "Jacksonian" democracy in practice. The Russian system is "Jeffersonian" in insisting on an aristocracy of excellence.

Higher education is, for many Americans, no more than an illustration of a high standard of living. It inundates the universities with many students of little ability and less scholarly eagerness who prevent the real students from getting a good education. Until we take education as seriously as we do the ever-more pretentious "thruways" for our automobiles and combine a generous scholarship program with more rigorous college entrance requirements, the Russian advantage over us is likely to be permanent.

We can, of course, console ourselves with the comforting and true reflection that this is the only despotism of history which requires efficiency for its survival; and technical efficiency requires brains which may prove themselves ultimately—but only *very* ultimately—incompatible with tyranny.

3. We were led astray by the fantastic Lysenko official biology of the Stalin era and imagined that science could not prosper in a dictatorship. The humanities and the arts in general feel the restraining power of the rulers who demand conformity to their standards of "social realism," for this means painting this false utopia according to the illusions of the oligarchs. But the pure scientists are apolitical, and have always been— whether here, or in Russia, or in Nazi Germany. Our earth satellite succeeded, among other reasons, because the Army had a brilliant young German rocketeer by the name of Wernher von Braun. He learned his trade under Hitler, where some of the Russian-German scientists also learned theirs.

The technical advances in Russia are the more inevitable because bright young people, anxious to be co-opted as junior partners of the oligarchy which controls Russia, will go into pure science rather than into the humanities where they are bound to bow their knee to the Baal of the dictatorship. In pure science and in technology the ambitions of the scientists and the ambitions of the oligarchs for international prestige coincide.

We were probably most grievously in error in the complacency with which we equated all kinds of freedom: the freedom of science, of conscience, of religion, of enterprise and the freedom to buy a new model automobile every year. In short, our indiscriminate freedom and our tremendous productivity have made our culture soft and vulgar, equating joy with happiness and happiness with comfort.

We have in fact become so self-indulgent that one may raise the question whether our position vis-à-vis the Russian is not the old historic situation: the "barbarians," hardy and disciplined, are ready to defeat a civilization in which the very achievements of its technology have made for soft and indulgent living. We in the churches must confess that we never pressed as much as we ought the truth of the scriptural precept that "life consisteth not in the abundance of things a man possesses." We are just as effete, and probably are more vulgar, than the Byzantines when the Moslems took Constantinople. The Communists are just as strong, fanatic and disciplined as the hordes of Islam were. Analogies are always inexact, but taken with caution they do teach us some lessons.

On second thought, the analogy is very misleading. That fracas between the Byzantines and the Moslems was a war to the death. There cannot be war between us without mutual annihilation. There must not be war. There can only be competitive co-existence. The competition is for the loyalty of the uncommitted nations of Asia and Africa. But in that war we must be reconciled to a great disadvantage. Our vaunted living standards are extravagant and odious to the imagination of the Asians and Africans. Our treasured democracy is really a necessity of justice, but on the colored continents it will appear to be an unattainable luxury, for a delicate balancing of social forces is required to make justice the end product of democracy. How much easier to slip from the organic collectivism of the past to the technical collectivism which promises efficiency and hides the fact that it also creates tyranny.

Original Sources of the Nine Essays

1. "The Challenge of the World Crisis"
   This essay is the first part of a paper, "Our Moral and Spiritual Resources for International Co-operation," written by Reinhold Niebuhr for the Fifth National Conference of the U. S. National Commission for UNESCO, held in November, 1955.

2. "America's Moral and Spiritual Resources"
   This is a slightly abridged version of the second part of the same UNESCO paper.

3. "Why Is Communism So Evil?"
   Written for Reinhold Niebuhr's book, *Christian Realism and Political Problems* (New York: Charles Scribner's Sons, 1953), this essay also appeared in *The New Leader,* June 8, 1953.

4. "The Anatomy of American Nationalism"
   This essay first appeared in *The New Leader,* February 28, 1955.

5. "The United Nations and the Free World"
   This essay was first published as a pamphlet, *The Moral Implications of Loyalty to the United Nations,* by the Edward W. Hazen Foundation, New Haven, Connecticut, in July, 1952.

6. "The Illusion of World Government"
   This essay first appeared in *Foreign Affairs,* April, 1949.

7. "The Limits of Cultural Co-operation"
   This essay is a part of a larger article which first appeared in *Christianity and Crisis,* October 17, 1949 (Vol. 9, No. 17), under the title, "Peace Through Cultural Co-operation."

8. "The Limits of Military Power"
   This essay first appeared in *The New Leader,* May 30, 1955.

9. "What We Can Learn from Sputnik"
   This essay originally appeared under the title, "After Sputnik and Explorer," in *Christianity and Crisis,* March 4, 1958 (Vol. 18, No. 4).